The Natural Laxative Cookbook

Karin Cadwell, Ph.D., R.N. & Edith White, M. Ed.

Foreword by Mark Donowitz, M.D.

Johns Hopkins University

Sterling Publishing Co., Inc.   New York

Acknowledgments

We want to acknowledge our many friends and family members who generously gave us their encouragement and support as we worked on this project.

We want especially to acknowledge the dedication and hard work of our two assistants, Anna Linnea Cadwell and Ruth Maas McIlhenny.

Library of Congress Cataloging-in-Publication Data

Cadwell, Karin.
   The natural laxative cookbook / by Karin Cadwell and Edith White ; with a foreword by Mark Donowitz.
      p.   cm.
   Includes index.
   ISBN 0-8069-1344-4
    1. Constipation—Diet therapy—Recipes. 2. High-fiber diet—Recipes. I. White, Edith. II. Title.
RC861.C23 1995
616.3'4280654—dc20   95-1230
                                              CIP

10 9 8 7 6 5 4 3 2

Published by Sterling Publishing Company, Inc.
387 Park Avenue South, New York, N.Y. 10016
© 1995 by Karin Cadwell and Edith White
Distributed in Canada by Sterling Publishing
% Canadian Manda Group, One Atlantic Avenue, Suite 105
Toronto, Ontario, Canada M6K 3E7
Distributed in Great Britain and Europe by Cassell PLC
Wellington House, 125 Strand, London WC2R 0BB, England
Distributed in Australia by Capricorn Link (Australia) Pty Ltd.
P.O. Box 6651, Baulkham Hills, Business Centre,
NSW 2153, Australia

Sterling ISBN 0-8069-1344-4

Contents

Foreword

Take a walk through the aisles of your local drug store and look at the variety of over-the-counter medications available for gastroenteric conditions. You'll notice that the number of different laxatives being sold far exceeds the number of other types of preparations, including the remedies for heartburn and acid indigestion. There are so many powders, tablets, and liquids claiming to be the "best" source of relief for constipation—not to mention the therapies that can "keep you regular for the rest of your life"—that it's almost overwhelming.

Why are there so many laxatives being marketed? The obvious explanation is that many, many people will suffer the discomforts of constipation during the course of their lives. Constipation appears to be a normal consequence of growing older. Three things happen as we age that can explain why this occurs: 1) The muscles that are part of our intestines weaken, reducing their efficiency. It is these muscles that are responsible for propelling contents through the small and large intestine. 2) The number of cells we have that create the intestinal water necessary for proper digestion and bowel movements decreases. Incredibly, the gastrointestinal tract is exposed to 9 liters of water each day. Only 2 liters come from drinking, the rest is secreted during digestion. Each organ in the gastrointestinal system—the salivary glands, stomach, small and large intestine, pancreas, liver and biliary system—plays a part in this secretion. Since 65%–85% of stool is made up of water, this reduction in intestinal water secretion contributes to constipation. 3) Regular exercise promotes the efficiency of our intestinal system by causing the abdominal muscles to contract, which assists in the muscle pumping that moves food through the intestines. Naturally, as we age, we become less active and therefore more likely to become constipated. Almost certainly, there are still explanations for age-related bowel problems yet to be discovered, as well as for the problems occurring in younger adults and even children.

Can true relief be found within any of the packages of laxatives sold in every drug store and supermarket? Unfortunately, when used chronically, many of the most widely available types of laxatives can damage the nerves and muscle of the intestine. This actually worsens the constipation and leads to even more reliance on the medications. Anyone suffering from frequent constipation should consult a doctor. Many serious illnesses can have constipation as a major symptom, including cancer of the colon, colitis, hypothyroidism, and diabetes. It can also be a side effect of many medications. Once such factors are ruled out, a physician can help a patient develop a healthy bowel maintenance plan that does not use those laxatives that are harmful to the system. One part of the management of constipation should surely include changes in diet.

The Natural Laxative Cookbook, by Karin Cadwell, Ph.D., R.N., and Edith White, M.Ed., is a clear and accurate resource for controlling constipation with a high-fiber diet and the use of plenty of fruits and vegetables. Such foods naturally contain substances that cause the intestine to secrete more water and increase intestinal motility, thereby promoting regular bowel movements.

The large number of tempting recipes provided in this handy cookbook make dietary management of constipation appealing, easy, and delicious.

Mark Donowitz, M.D.
Paulson Professor of Medicine
Chief, Division of Gastroenterology
Johns Hopkins University School of Medicine
Baltimore, Maryland

Introduction

This cookbook is full of recipes with ingredients that act as natural laxatives, such as prunes and bran cereals. It is aimed primarily at helping people avoid constipation. It is based on the idea that it is better to eat a variety of healthy foods than to rely on laxative products. Actually, eating good ("laxative") foods is not only helpful for constipation, but is associated with better health in other areas. These include weight control, diabetes, heart disease, cancer, diverticulitis, colitis, and irritable bowel syndrome.

Constipation

Constipation is defined as the passage of hard, dry feces. It is likely to happen to people who fail to eat enough laxative-quality foods. It also happens to people who fail to drink enough fluids. Constipation can also happen to people who ignore the urge to defecate, which can also cause stools become hard and dry.

Certain medications and dietary supplements, such as narcotic pain-killers, anti-depressants, iron pills, or aluminum-containing antacids can also lead to constipation. Additionally, people who are immobilized after surgery often become constipated.

Constipation can also be a sign of a serious medical problem. If you notice a change in bowel habits, discuss it with your health-care provider. If you already have a medical problem, such as diverticulitis or diabetes, do not change your diet without first talking it over with your health-care provider. Ask if a high-fiber diet is good for you.

Understanding the Term "Fiber"

It helps to understand words such as "fiber." We hear about fiber on television and we see it listed on food labels, such as boxes of bran cereals. But what does it mean?

Fiber, which used to be called roughage, describes a part of plants. Only foods of plant origin have fiber, and they don't all have the same amount. Raspberries, for example, have more than cherries. Animal-derived foods, such as meat or eggs or milk, have no fiber.

Beans, nuts, fruits and vegetables, and whole grain products tend to be high-fiber foods.

There are two different types of fiber: soluble and insoluble. Some, such as oat bran, are water-soluble. These have been shown to lower the levels of cholesterol in the blood. Hence the popularity of oat bran. Other types, such as wheat bran, are insoluble; they are not water-soluble. These soften the stool and add bulk to it. Remember this: oat bran to lower cholesterol; wheat bran or rice bran to prevent constipation.

The fiber content of a food is not changed by what we do to it. Cooking a carrot does not decrease its fiber content. Toasting a piece of bread and making it crispier does not increase its fiber content. How crunchy a food is has nothing to do with its fiber content. Crusty French and Italian bread are fairly low in fiber. All breads made from white flour are fairly low in fiber, because the outer coat of the grain—the bran—has been removed. White bread is not a good source of fiber.

Human beings do not have the enzymes needed to break down fiber. We cannot burn it in the form of calories. We cannot store it as fat. So fiber passes through the intestinal tract and down to the colon in approximately the same form it was in when it was eaten. It is worthwhile even though we can't digest it. Actually, fiber is worthwhile *because* we can't digest it. As it passes through the intestinal system, it attracts and holds water. The result is that the end product of digestion—feces, or stool—is bulkier and softer and more easily passed when it is higher in fiber.

People who eat high-fiber foods have increased peristalsis. Peristalsis refers to the wavelike motions that move food onwards from the time it is swallowed and as it makes its way down the throat, through the stomach, and all along in the digestive tract. Increased peristalsis means that waste is moved out of the body faster.

The sensation of needing to have a bowel movement comes from the pressure of the weight of waste building up in the colon. This is a direct result of the amount of waste (especially fiber) in the food that was eaten.

The waste of the person on a low-fiber diet remains in the body for a longer time than that of a person on a high-fiber diet and some of the water is reabsorbed. The results are small stools that are hard to pass and a longer time between bowel movements. Also, when waste remains in the colon too long, problems can occur. If you are one of the many people who have been taking laxatives for years in order to have bowel movements, take note: Many people have been able to break the laxative habit by adding fiber to their diet.

In societies where people eat high-fiber diets, constipation is virtually unknown. In some "poor" countries there is no word in the native language for constipation. Not only does it not exist, but related problems, such as hemorrhoids, colon cancer, and diverticulitis, are also rare or nonexistent.

Years ago our great-grandparents lived on high-fiber diets. Then the standard Western diet changed. White bread had snob appeal, so the outer part of the whole wheat—the bran—was milled out. People began to eat more meat and dairy products. They ate fewer ethnic foods and bean dishes, dishes that are naturally high in fiber.

It is not difficult to change a typical low-fiber diet back to a high-fiber one. But it's wise to make changes gradually. You might start by eating more vegetables and more fresh or dried fruits. Leave the peel on your apples, potatoes, or cucumbers. Then eat a high-fiber breakfast cereal. Gradually include more beans.

Bran as Medicine

A few years ago wheat bran became *the* remedy for constipation. People were told to sprinkle a little wheat bran on their food. This was never an ideal solution. In fact, rice bran is more laxative than wheat bran. Also, people who take bran as medicine miss out on all the other nutrients in good foods. Apricots, for example, are not only a good source of fiber. They also have vitamins and beta-carotene.

There is another problem with just taking bran. Since it swells as it absorbs water, people who add it to their diets **must** remember to drink more liquids. Otherwise the added bran can be constipating or even dangerous. If you hear someone say: "Every time I eat high-fiber foods, I get more constipated," it's a sure sign the person isn't drinking enough water.

We remember a man who died while square dancing. People thought he died of a heart attack, but he didn't. The autopsy showed he had a grapefruit-sized bran obstruction in his intestine, which burst.

How did this happen? The man had started taking plain, dry bran, but without extra fluids. When he noticed his bowels weren't moving, he took even more bran. Again, he failed to drink enough fluids.

Mother Nature packages her healthy high-fiber foods with natural fluids. Raspberries and broccoli have natural fluids in them. When you eat bean soup, you get fluid along with the fiber in the beans. If you add bran to your diet, drink plenty of fluids. But remember, it is healthier to eat a variety of high-fiber foods than just to add bran to your diet.

There Is More to Laxative Action Than Just Fiber

Manufacturers of high-fiber foods have put a lot of money and effort into advertising the benefits of fiber. Certainly, high-fiber foods, such as bran cereals and baked beans, do act as natural laxatives. But there is more to laxatives than just fiber. Substances that are low or even lacking in fiber can act as laxatives. Water can be thought of as an ideal "natural laxative" food. Some people find that drinking a cup of hot water with half a lemon squeezed into it causes them to have a bowel movement. Some people drink coffee and soon feel the urge to defecate. Eating yogurt made with acidophilus cultures can also work as a laxative. (Read the labels on yogurt containers before you buy. Some brands of yogurt lack active cultures and are made with gelatin.)

Some people find that other foods fairly low in fiber act as natural laxatives. Some people swear by ripe bananas, while others use bananas to cure diarrhea. There do seem to be individual differences. Although the variety of rhubarb commonly found in grocery stores is less laxative than many others, some people find it to be quite effective nevertheless.

About Portion Sizes and Food Values

It has become common practice in recent years to standardize portion sizes. We have followed this convention and use standard portion sizes. But please be aware that these standard portions are smaller than what most people actually eat. For liquids, a portion is often listed as 8 ounces, or 250 mL. If you get out your drinking glasses and a measure them, you'll probably find they hold much more.

A standard serving of meat is about the size of the smallest (or child-size) hamburger patty at a fast-food restaurant. In real life, most people serve and eat much larger portions of meat. If you eat a generous serving of meat, you'll probably eat at least twice that amount. So you'll get twice the number of calories and twice the amount of cholesterol, saturated fat, and sodium.

Cookbooks and magazines sometimes publish photographs of generous servings while listing the food values for the standard (some would say skimpy) portions. Perhaps people have been happy to go along with the small-portion convention because of the good (low) scores recipes get with calories, cholesterol, saturated fat, and sodium; these "bad" components should get low scores, as in a golf game.

But with fiber, the good scores are more like basketball. People want the numbers to look as high as possible. When we use the small-portion convention, our fiber scores look less impressive than if we admitted we probably eat more than the portion size listed.

Actually, the fiber score on a small serving of any individual recipe should not look super-high. The point is to eat many different laxative-quality foods throughout the day. With natural laxative cooking, no one food is supposed to act like Ex-Lax and be a super-purgative.

The Goal Is Good Health for the Entire Body, Not Just the Elimination System

There is increasing evidence that eating a high-fiber, low-fat diet can help prevent overweight, heart disease, certain cancers, and intestinal problems such as colitis and diverticulitis.

How do high-fiber foods help prevent overweight? Actually, in several ways:

First, high-fiber foods are fairly low in calories. Ounce for ounce, blueberries have one-tenth the calories of chocolate bars. Unbuttered popcorn is so low in calories we can eat 10 cups of it for the same number of calories one doughnut has. Many of us admit to liking chocolate bars and doughnuts, despite their high calorie and fat content. What we need to do is find healthy but delicious alternatives.

Also, most high-fiber foods are naturally low in fat. Beans have much less fat than hamburger, so using them in chili instead of hamburger reduces the calories.

Also, high-fiber foods need a lot of chewing. Certainly 10 cups of popcorn would take a long time to chew. The more you chew, the more slowly you eat. The more slowly you eat, the less you eat before you feel full. And since part of the reason for eating and snacking is to satisfy an urge to munch, high fiber, low-fat foods chewed slowly and thoroughly more than meet that need. Finally, a high-fiber diet can prevent constipation. Many people who do not eat high-fiber foods while dieting get constipated.

Heart disease is still the number-one killer in Western nations. Not only can oat bran help reduce cholesterol, but by eating other high-fiber foods, such as beans, you eat less meat. This is a natural way to cut down on the saturated fat and cholesterol found in red meat.

When you eat lots of grains, fruits, and vegetables, you are less likely to heap on excess salt. By going easier on the salt, you'll get more of the valuable potassium in fruits and vegetables. This in turn can help keep blood pressure within the normal range. Other factors, such as getting enough exercise and avoiding cigarette smoking and stress, come into the picture, but don't minimize the impact of a good diet on your health and well-being.

Diabetes is another serious health problem associated with diet. Researchers have found that many diabetics can control their blood sugar better if they eat more high-fiber foods. Certain types of fiber seem particularly helpful. These include pectins (found in ripe fruits) and gums, especially guar gum (found in beans and lentils). The fiber in beans moderates the insulin response by taking longer to digest. Refined sugar, on the other hand, enters the bloodstream very quickly, and a great deal of insulin is necessary to deal with it.

It is extremely important for any diabetic to talk to his/her doctor, nurse practitioner, or dietitian before changing the diet. If high-fiber foods are recommended, try beans, lentils, and vegetables. One word of warning: This is *not* a cookbook for diabetics, and some recipes do contain sugar, corn syrup, or foods with a lot of concentrated natural sugar, such as dried fruits.

Another word of warning: This is not a cookbook for people with diverticulitis or colitis. Be sure to avoid ingredients that bother you, be they seeds, nuts, or anything else.

Readers who wish to cut down on salt or sodium can do it in several ways with the recipes in this cookbook. One way is simply to omit the salt altogether. Another is to avoid all canned foods except those labelled salt-free. (Canned fruits are naturally salt free.) Cook dry beans from scratch, instead of using canned beans. For people who like the convenience of using canned beans, vegetables, tuna, and other fish, a compromise is to empty the contents of the can into a colander, rinse thoroughly, and drain.

Pregnant Women Often Become Constipated

Pregnant women, of course, should consult an obstetrician or other health-care provider about their health concerns. Chances are they will be told to drink plenty of water and eat a variety of healthy, high-fiber foods. So the recipes in this cookbook are ideal for pregnant women.

Pyramids That Help Us Remember Which Foods to Eat

For years, nutritionists and others have tried to simplify the teaching of foods so that people would eat the right amounts of various foods. Now it's the food pyramid of the United States Department of Agriculture that's used.

We offer here our own Natural Laxative Pyramid. It lists foods in the same pyramid sections as the regular USDA pyramid. But here we list only laxative foods. Obviously, many other healthy foods should be included in your diet, but if you take a copy of the Natural Laxative Pyramid to the store with you, it can remind you which foods to buy.

But Isn't There a Problem with Beans and Some Vegetables?

The problem is flatulence, or gas. Perhaps this is one reason why many people shy away from beans and other high-fiber foods. What can you do? You can introduce such foods gradually and make a habit of eating them, because when gassy foods are eaten regularly, the body gets used to them. Problems with gas almost disappear after a few weeks.

In the meantime, another suggestion is to use a product called Beano. Beano is a food enzyme that helps break down complex, indigestible sugars from many gassy foods into simple, digestible ones. Adding Beano drops to your first bite of gassy food can cut down on the problem. The standard recommendation is to add 3–8 drops to a half-cup serving of gassy food. If you're having broiled fish, a baked potato, and half a cup of broccoli, a few drops of Beano would be enough. But for baked beans and cole slaw you would

The Natural Laxative Pyramid

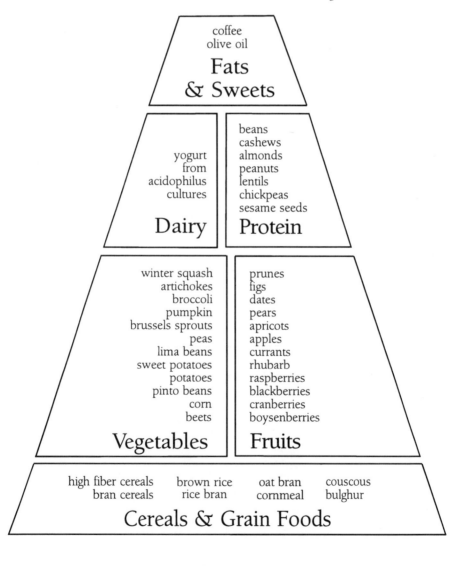

coffee
olive oil
Fats & Sweets

yogurt
from
acidophilus
cultures

Dairy

beans
cashews
almonds
peanuts
lentils
chickpeas
sesame seeds

Protein

winter squash
artichokes
broccoli
pumpkin
brussels sprouts
peas
lima beans
sweet potatoes
potatoes
pinto beans
corn
beets

Vegetables

prunes
figs
dates
pears
apricots
apples
currants
rhubarb
raspberries
blackberries
cranberries
boysenberries

Fruits

high fiber cereals   brown rice   oat bran   couscous
bran cereals   rice bran   cornmeal   bulghur

Cereals & Grain Foods

need more. Experiment and see how much Beano you need to use. It's also available in tablet form, with the recommendation to chew two or three tablets before eating the first mouthful of food, which should be enough for a normal meal of two or three servings of gassy foods.

The recipes in this cookbook do, unashamedly, call for a lot of beans, fruits, and vegetables. We hope you will make these laxative recipes part of a good, well-balanced diet. And please remember to drink lots of fluids. And, of course, check with your own health care provider about your individual health concerns.

Chapter 1: Breakfast

Many of the most convenient "laxative" foods are commonly eaten at breakfast. Cold and hot cereals made from bran are widely available. Labels on cereal boxes tell us their fiber content, which can be used as a guide to how laxative the cereal will be. A very high fiber cereal may have 15 grams of fiber in a (small) one-ounce serving. Cereals with moderately high fiber may have 7 grams per one-ounce serving. So the person who is rushed in the morning can simply put a high-fiber cold cereal into a bowl and add fruit. The most laxative fruits are dried prunes and figs. Dried apricots, dates, apples, or raisins can also be kept on hand. Good fresh fruit choices are slices of apple or pear (preferably unpeeled) and berries. These include raspberries, blueberries, or other locally available berries such as boysenberries. Slices of peach, mango, or banana are other options.

On days when there is a little more time, high-fiber pancakes are a good choice. Instead of adding syrup, add a fruit topping. This chapter has recipes for several choices. If time at breakfast is limited, make them up ahead of time and simply reheat them for a hot pancake topping.

Omelettes can be made with either eggs or egg substitutes for those who need to lower their cholesterol. Many traditional omelette ingredients are binding (cheese, meat), but laxative ingredients can be added. These include leftover cooked broccoli or pieces of fruit. Many people have found that their morning cup of coffee signals their body to have a bowel movement. In hot weather some people like to drink a nutritious cold beverage. We offer a couple of delicious cold drinks that are quite laxative.

Granola

Apple juice replaces oil to make this granola recipe much lower in calories.

3 C	oatmeal (regular)	750 mL
¼ C	oat bran	60 mL
¼ C	wheat germ	60 mL
⅔ C	almonds, sliced, unsalted	180 mL
1 T	olive oil	15 mL
¼ C	light corn syrup	60 mL
2 T	molasses	30 mL
¼ C	apple juice	60 mL

Mix the oatmeal, oat bran, wheat germ, and almonds in a flat lasagna pan or a jelly roll pan. In a saucepan, combine and heat oil, corn syrup, molasses, and apple juice. Drizzle over the oatmeal mixture; use a spatula to push the mixture around in the pan. Bake at 325°F (165°C) for about 30 minutes. Then, mix again and bake for 10 minutes. (The longer it cooks, the crunchier it gets.) *Yield: 9 servings*

Calories per serving: 228
Total fat: 8.6 g
Saturated fat: 1.12 g
Cholesterol: 0 mg
Fiber: 2.33 g
Sodium: 9.5 mg

Steamed Dried Fruit

Use any dried fruit or any combination of dried fruits.

Wash the dried fruit. Steam it in a colander, steamer basket, or coarse strainer held over a kettle of boiling water. Do not let the water touch the fruit. Cover tightly and steam until the fruit is plump and tender.

Breakfast Fruit Treat
Quick and easy for a great breakfast on the go.

2 C	pecans, chopped in an electric blender	500 mL
1 T	wheat germ	15 mL
1	apple, unpeeled, cored, and finely diced	1
1	banana, sliced	1
1	pear, unpeeled, cored	1
1 C	raisins	250 mL
1 t	molasses	5 mL
1 C	yogurt	250 mL

Combine the ingredients, except the yogurt. Fold in the yogurt.
Yield: 6 servings

Calories per serving: 392	Cholesterol: 0 mg
Total fat: 24.9 g	Fiber: 6.32 g
Saturated fat: 2.06 g	Sodium: 28.4 mg

Fig and Apricot Conserve
Make this ahead for a change from the usual breakfast fruit.

½ C	corn syrup	125 mL
1½ C	water	375 mL
1 C	dried apricots, halved	250 mL
½ C	raisins	125 mL
½ t	anise seeds (optional)	2 mL
1	lemon, juiced	1

In a saucepan, boil the corn syrup and water. Add the remaining ingredients and simmer for 25 minutes. Stir occasionally. Serve hot or chilled in custard cups. *Yield: 10 servings*

Calories per serving: 289	Cholesterol: 0 mg
Total fat: 0.8 g	Fiber: 10.05 g
Saturated fat: 0.17 g	Sodium: 20.2 mg

Sweet Stewed Prunes

Prunes are a very good laxative and this recipe makes them taste elegant. Make up a batch and store them in the refrigerator.

6 oz	dried pitted prunes	185 mL
1 C	pineapple juice, unsweetened	250 mL
1	lemon slice, thin	1
3	cloves, whole	3
⅛ t	nutmeg, freshly grated or ground	.5 mL

Place the ingredients in a small saucepan. Bring to a boil. Reduce heat, cover, and simmer for 15 minutes. Cool completely in an uncovered saucepan. Discard cloves before serving. *Yield: 4 servings*

Calories per serving: 116   Cholesterol: 0 mg
Total fat: 0.4 g   Fiber: 3.20 g
Saturated fat: 0.10 g   Sodium: 4.5 mg

Rhubarb and Blueberry Compote

A great recipe during fresh-rhubarb season.

1 lb	rhubarb, peeled and cut into 2″ slices	480 g
½ C	brown sugar	125 mL
½ t	nutmeg	2 mL
1 T	lemon juice	15 mL
1 T	orange peel, grated	15 mL
2 C	blueberries, fresh or frozen	500 mL
1 C	white grape juice	250 mL

Combine all ingredients in a medium saucepan. Simmer, covered, for 20 to 25 minutes, or until rhubarb is tender. Add more sugar to taste. Refrigerate and serve cold with cereal, yogurt, or both! *Yield: 6 servings*

Calories per serving: 146   Cholesterol: 0 mg
Total fat: 0.5 g   Fiber: 3.09 g
Saturated fat: 0.07 g   Sodium: 14.6 mg

Breakfast Squares

You'll be surprised to see beans disguised in this cakelike breakfast. For smaller families, make a pan on the weekend and eat it all week.

4	eggs or equivalent egg substitute	4
1 C	olive oil	250 mL
1 C	corn syrup	250 mL
2 C	white kidney or cannellini beans, cooked or canned, drained, and pureed	500 mL
2 t	baking soda	10 mL
1 C	flour	250 mL
2 t	cinnamon	10 mL
1 t	ginger	5 mL
½ t	nutmeg	2 mL
1 C	pecans, chopped	250 mL
2 C	carrots, grated	500 mL
1 C	apricots, chopped finely	250 mL

Beat the eggs or egg substitute in the large bowl of an electric mixer. Add the corn syrup slowly while beating. Beat the oil into the egg mixture. Mix in the bean puree, baking soda, flour, cinnamon, ginger, and nutmeg. Fold in the nuts, apricots, and carrots. Bake in 350°F (175°C) oven in a 9 × 13 inch (23 × 33 cm) pan for about 70 minutes. Cool on a wire rack. Frosting is optional. *Yield: 12 servings*

Calories per serving: 410	Cholesterol: 0 mg
Total fat: 24.4 g	Fiber: 3.11 g
Saturated fat: 0.56 g	Sodium: 253.8 mg

Apple and Apricot Omelet

Add fiber to your omelet in this easy and delicious way.

¾ C	water	190 mL
1	apple, cored, chopped	1
¼ C	apricots, dried, chopped	60 mL
¼ t	cinnamon	1 mL
4	eggs, or equivalent egg substitute, lightly beaten	4
1 T	yogurt	15 mL
	black pepper, to taste	
1 t	water	5 mL
1 T	olive oil	15 mL

Combine the water, apple, apricots, and cinnamon in a small saucepan. Cook over medium-low heat until liquid is absorbed. Stir occasionally. Beat the eggs or egg substitute, yogurt, pepper, and water in a large bowl. In a large skillet, heat the oil. Pour in the egg mixture and cook over medium heat until the bottom sets, letting the egg run under the edges. Top with fruit mixture. Fold over the omelet. *Yield: 4 servings*

Calories per serving: 95
Total fat: 3.7 g
Saturated fat: 0.62 g

Cholesterol: 0.9 mg
Fiber: 0.93 g
Sodium: 133.6 mg

Corncakes with Maple-Yogurt Topping

Once you try these corncakes, you'll want to make them every day.

Corncakes

¾ C	stone-ground cornmeal	190 mL
½ C	all-purpose white flour	125 mL
½ C	whole wheat flour	125 mL
1 t	baking powder	5 mL
1 T	sugar	15 mL
1 C	nonfat milk	250 mL
½ C	low-fat or nonfat yogurt	125 mL
2 T	olive oil	30 mL
4	egg whites	4

Topping

1 C	nonfat yogurt	250 mL
⅓ C	maple syrup	90 mL

To make the corncakes: Combine the dry ingredients in a large bowl. In a medium-sized bowl, mix milk, yogurt, and oil. Blend into cornmeal mixture. Beat egg whites until stiff peaks form and fold into batter. In a medium-hot pan coated with non-stick cooking spray, fry pancakes until brown and puffed on each side, about 5 minutes. *Yield: 6 servings*

To make the topping: Combine ingredients in a small bowl. Spoon over the pancakes. *Yield: 6 servings*

Calories per serving of corncakes: 212	Cholesterol: 0.7 mg
Total fat: 5.1 g	Fiber: 1.98 g
Saturated fat: 0.69 g	Sodium: 133.0 mg

Calories per serving of topping: 79	Cholesterol: 0 mg
Total fat: 0 g	Fiber: 0 g
Saturated fat: 0 g	Sodium: 26.2 mg

Blueberry Pancakes

These pancakes are fantastic! They're so flavorful, you'll prefer them to your old recipe!

¾ C	whole wheat flour	190 mL
½ t	baking soda	15 mL
1 pinch	salt	1 pinch
1 t	cream of tartar	5 mL
½ C	wheat germ	125 mL
2	egg whites	2
1 C	nonfat milk	250 mL
3 t	canola oil	15 mL
½ C	blueberries	125 mL

Mix the flour, baking soda, cream of tartar, and wheat germ. Make a well in the center. Drop in the egg whites, milk, and oil. Mix until smooth. Cook in a heated frying pan coated with non-stick cooking spray. Use 2 T batter for each pancake. Sprinkle a few blueberries onto each pancake as it cooks. Cook until bubbles form in the surface. Turn and cook until the other side is brown. *Yield: 12*

Calories per serving: 78
Total fat: 4.0 g
Saturated fat: 0.33 g

Cholesterol: 0.3 mg
Fiber: 1.37 g
Sodium: 66.3 mg

Oat Bran Pancakes

Oat bran is famous for lowering serum cholesterol, and these pancakes really make good health delicious.

1 C	Oat bran hot cereal, uncooked	250 mL
½ C	whole wheat flour	125 mL
1 t	sugar	5 mL
2 t	baking powder	10 mL
1 C	nonfat milk	250 mL
1 T	vegetable oil	15 mL
1	egg white, slightly beaten	1

Combine the oat bran, flour, sugar, and baking powder. In another bowl, combine the remaining ingredients. Pour wet mixture into dry mixture and mix until moistened. For each pancake pour ½ cup batter onto a griddle heated medium-high and coated with non-stick cooking spray. Turn pancakes when bubbles form on the surface. Serve with fruit topping. *Yield: 4 servings*

Calories per serving: 200 Cholesterol: 1.0 mg
Total fat: 5.1 g Fiber: 0.33 g
Saturated fat: 0.53 g Sodium: 241.3 mg

Fruit Topping

Using a fruit topping instead of pancake syrup not only adds a lot more flavor, it also boosts the laxative power of your breakfast.

¼ C	apple or white grape juice, unsweetened	60 mL
1½ t	cornstarch	7 mL
1 C	berries, or other fruit, fresh or unsweetened frozen	250 mL

Stir the juice and cornstarch. Pour over the fruit in the saucepan. Heat over medium-low heat until thickened. Stir occasionally. Add nutmeg or other spices if desired. Serve hot over frozen yogurt or pancakes. *Yield: 4 (¼ C/60 mL) servings*

Calories per serving: 26 Cholesterol: 0 mg
Total fat: 0.2 g Fiber: 1.52 g
Saturated fat: 0.01 g Sodium: 0.4 mg

Fruit Sauce to Top Pancakes or Yogurt or Angel Cake

1½ C	fresh or frozen raspberries	375 mL
4 t	sugar	20 mL
1 T	lemon juice	15 mL

Blend one-half cup (125 mL) fruit with sugar and lemon juice until smooth. Add the remaining fruit, and stir mixture. *Yield: 5 servings*

Calories per serving: 31
Total fat: 0.2 g
Saturated fat: 0.01 g

Cholesterol: 0 mg
Fiber: 1.82 g
Sodium: 0.6 mg

Hot Cider and Cranberry Juice

For some people, a warm breakfast fruit drink makes all the laxative difference.

1 qt	apple cider	1 L
1 qt	cranberry juice	1 L
2 T	brown sugar	30 mL
2	cinnamon sticks	2
½ t	whole cloves	2 mL

Bring ingredients to a boil. Simmer 15 minutes. Strain. Serve in mugs. This keeps very well in the refrigerator and improves when reheated. *Yield: 12 servings*

Calories per serving: 96
Total fat: 0.2 g
Saturated fat: 0.02 g

Cholesterol: 0 mg
Fiber: 0.15 g
Sodium: 4.8 mg

Breakfast Fruity

Perfect for people who don't have much morning appetite.

1	banana	1
1	apple, cored	1
1	pear, cored	1
¾ C	orange juice	190 mL
2 t	raisins	10 mL

Blend the ingredients in an electric blender until smooth. Makes a thick drink. *Yield: 2 servings*

Calories per serving: 215
Total fat: 0.9 g
Saturated fat: 0.19 g

Cholesterol: 0 mg
Fiber: 6.13 g
Sodium: 2.3 mg

Cranberry Breakfast Drink

Fresh cranberries add protection to the urinary tract. Defrosted cranberries can be substituted.

2 C	fresh cranberries	500 mL
1 C	water	250 mL
1 C	orange juice (or another juice)	250 mL
½ C	light corn syrup	125 mL

Blend until liquefied. Chill before serving. *Yield: 4 servings*

Calories per serving: 174
Total fat: 0.1 g
Saturated fat: 0.01 g

Cholesterol: 0 mg
Fiber: 2.06 g
Sodium: 28.3 mg

Icy Mango Drink
A laxative power drink!

¼ C	orange juice	60 mL
1 C	fresh mango, peeled, seeded, and chopped	250 mL
½ t	sugar, or to taste	2 mL
2 t	lime juice, fresh	10 mL
4	ice cubes	4

Combine all the ingredients in a blender or food processor until smooth. *Yield: 2 servings*

Calories per serving: 86
Total fat: 0.3 g
Saturated fat: 0.07 g

Cholesterol: 0 mg
Fiber: 2.11 g
Sodium: 2.3 mg

Chapter 2: Snacks

Red Bean Dip

With canned beans you can put this dip together in no time. For the lowest sodium content use cooked dried beans. You can drastically reduce the sodium content of canned beans by putting them in a colander and washing them under cold running water.

¼ C	ketchup	60 mL
2 T	cider vinegar	30 mL
dash	Tabasco sauce (more if you like it hotter)	dash
¼ t	liquid hickory smoke	1 mL
1 t	garlic powder	5 mL
3 C	kidney beans canned, drained	750 mL
1	small onion	1
	salt and pepper, to taste (optional)	

Blend all the ingredients in a food processor or blender until smooth. Scrape into small jars or bowls, and chill. At serving time, garnish with parsley, cucumber slices, scallions, cherry tomatoes, or whatever vegetables are in season. *Yield: 24 servings*

Calories: 32	Cholesterol: 0 mg
Total fat: 0.1 g	Fiber: 1.01 g
Saturated fat: 0.02 g	Sodium: 135.7 mg

Hummus

A traditional Mediterranean food high in fiber from chickpeas, which are combined with yogurt.

1	garlic clove	1
½	onion	½
15 oz	can chickpeas, drained	430 mL
½ C	nonfat yogurt	125 mL
	freshly ground black pepper and garlic powder, to taste	

Mash the garlic and onion in a food processor or blender. Add the chickpeas and puree. Gradually beat in the yogurt and continue until well combined. Add pepper and garlic powder to taste. Transfer to a serving dish, cover, and chill for 30 minutes. Serve with high-fiber crackers or whole wheat pita bread. *Yield: 4 servings*

Calories: 129
Total fat: 2.0 g
Saturated fat: 0.71 g

Cholesterol: 3.6 mg
Fiber: 3.40 g
Sodium: 282.7 mg

Baked Bean Dip

If beans give you gas, sprinkle a few drops of Beano on the first bite of this easy-to-make dip.

1	onion, quartered	1
½	green pepper, cut in pieces	½
1 lb	baked beans, canned, drained	.45 kg
1½ t	horseradish (optional)	7 mL

Use a blender or food processor to chop the onion and green pepper. Combine with the baked beans and horseradish (optional). To make the dip hot, add 2 to 3 hot chili peppers. Blend to a smooth paste. *Yield: 16 servings*

Calories: 43
Total fat: 0.3 g
Saturated fat: 0 g

Cholesterol: 0 mg
Fiber: 1.88 g
Sodium: 55.7 mg

Pinto Bean Dip
This bean dip has a sweet-and-sour flavor.

1 T	olive oil	15 mL
1	medium onion, diced	1
1	clove garlic, minced	1
dash	liquid hickory smoke	dash
1 t	no-salt chili powder	5 mL
dash	Tabasco sauce	dash
2 C	pinto beans canned, drained	500 mL
2 T	vinegar (cider is best)	30 mL
1 T	sugar	15 mL
	salt and pepper, to taste	

Heat the oil in a skillet over medium heat and sauté the onion and garlic for a few minutes until soft. Add the hickory smoke, chili powder, and Tabasco sauce. Stir in the vinegar and sugar. Whip all together, with the pinto beans, in a food processor or blender until smooth. Correct the seasonings. Add more Tabasco sauce if you like a "hotter" flavor. Store, covered, in the refrigerator. *Yield: 8 servings*

Calories: 88	Cholesterol: 0 mg
Total fat: 2.1 g	Fiber: 5.10 g
Saturated fat: 0.30 g	Sodium: 11.7 mg

Yogurt Dip for Crudités
What could be easier? For laxative benefits, be sure to buy yogurt with acidophilus cultures.

1 (8 oz)	container of nonfat yogurt	1 (240 g)
2 T	mustard	30 mL

Using a wire whisk, combine ingredients. *Yield: 4 servings*

Calories: 32	Cholesterol: 0 mg
Total fat: 0.3 g	Fiber: 0.21 g
Saturated fat: 0.02 g	Sodium: 133.8 mg

Jalapeño Bean Dip
Use more peppers if you like a really spicy dip.

2	jalapeño peppers, small, pickled	2
1½ C	cooked pinto beans, mashed	375 mL
1 T	olive oil	15 mL
½ t	oregano	2 mL
¼ t	garlic powder	1 mL

Cut the tops off the peppers. Combine the whole peppers and remaining ingredients in a food processor or blender. Blend to a smooth paste. *Yield: 12 servings*

Calories: 40
Total fat: 1.3 g
Saturated fat: 0.18 g

Cholesterol: 0 mg
Fiber: 2.39 g
Sodium: 17.0 mg

Prune Tsimmes
Lois Ambash suggested this recipe. Tsimmes is a Yiddish word that refers to a side dish of mixed cooked vegetables and fruits, slightly seasoned.

½ pound	pitted prunes	250 g
½ pound	dried apricots	250 g
4 C	water	1 L
6	carrots, peeled and diced	6
2 T	lemon juice	10 mL
1 C	ginger snap cookie crumbs	250 mL
handful	raisins or frozen peas (optional)	handful

Place all the ingredients in a large pot. Cover and simmer over a low heat for about 30 minutes. Stir often to avoid sticking. Serve as a side dish or with matzoh crackers as an appetizer. *Yield: 12 ½ cup (125 ml) servings*

Calories per serving: 156
Total fat: 1 g
Saturated fat: 0 g

Cholesterol: 0 mg
Fiber: 2 g
Sodium: 74 mg

Guacamole Dip
Florida avocados are higher in fiber than others.

1	large Florida avocado	1
2 t	lime or lemon juice	10 mL
½ t	garlic powder	2 mL
½ t	onion powder	2 mL
dash	Tabasco sauce	dash

Slice the avocado in half; remove the seed. Using a spoon, scoop out the avocado flesh. Place the avocado, lime or lemon juice, and seasonings in a food processor or blender. Use the mixing blade of the processor and pulse gently to mash the avocado. If you use a blender, be careful that the mixture does not liquefy. *Yield: 8 servings*

Calories: 45	Cholesterol: 0 mg
Total fat: 3.9 g	Fiber: 0.87 g
Saturated fat: 3.9 g	Sodium: 4.9 mg

Strawberry-Banana Dip
Serve this dip with wedges of unpeeled apple.

½ pint	strawberries	240 mL
1	banana, large, ripe	1
1 t	lemon juice	5 mL
dash	cinnamon or nutmeg	dash

Mash together the berries and banana. Sprinkle with lemon juice. Add the cinnamon or nutmeg and serve immediately. *Yield: 4 servings*

Calories per serving: 38	Cholesterol: 0 mg
Total fat: 0.3 g	Fiber: 1.39 g
Saturated fat: 0.06 g	Sodium: 0.8 mg

Baked Potato Skins

A tasty snack.

4	baking potatoes, baked in their skins	4
2 T	olive oil	30 mL
½ t	onion powder	2 mL
½ t	garlic powder	2 mL
½ t	paprika	2 mL

Cut the baked potatoes in half lengthwise and scoop out the insides, leaving a layer of potato near the skin. Mix the olive oil, onion powder, garlic powder, and paprika. Arrange the potato skins, insides up, on a cookie sheet. Brush with the flavored mixture. Bake at 400°F (200°C) oven for 15–20 minutes. *Yield: 8 servings*

Calories: 141
Total fat: 3.5 g
Saturated fat: 0.48 g

Cholesterol: 0 mg
Fiber: 2.06 g
Sodium: 8.2 mg

Bran Chex Snacks

Using high-fiber cereals from the grocery store is a very easy way to boost your laxative plan.

½ C	olive oil	125 mL
1 t	curry powder	5 mL
1 t	onion powder	5 mL
¼ t	ginger	1 mL
3 C	Bran Chex	750 mL

Heat the oil in a large frying pan and stir in the curry powder, onion powder, and ginger. Toss the Bran Chex in the seasoned oil and stir for 5 more minutes. *Yield: 3 cups (750 mL)*

Calories per ½ C (125 mL):
    250
Total fat: 18.85 g
Saturated fat: 2.43 g

Cholesterol: 0 mg
Fiber: 2.88 g
Sodium: 2.88 mg

Chocolate Bran Bars

Using bran cereals in baked goods makes them moist and delicious.

Bars

1 C	flour	250 mL
	salt, to taste	
¼ C	olive oil	60 mL
½ C	dark corn syrup	125 mL
1 t	vanilla	5 mL
2	eggs or equivalent egg substitute	2
2 C	bran flakes	500 mL
1 C	raisins	250 mL
½ C	walnuts, coarsely chopped	125 mL

Frosting

¾ C	chocolate chips	190 mL

To make the bars: Combine the flour and salt. In another bowl, combine the oil and corn syrup. Add the vanilla and eggs to the liquid combination, and beat well. Stir in the bran flakes, raisins, and nuts. Add the flour mixture. Spread mixture in a well-greased 9-inch (23 cm) square pan. Bake at 350°F (175°C) for 30 minutes. **For the frosting:** Sprinkle chips on top while hot. Let sit for three minutes. Spread the melted chocolate and cut into bars. *Yield: 18 bars*

Calories per bar: 143   Cholesterol: 0 mg
Total fat: 4.8 g   Fiber: 1.75 g
Saturated fat: 0.57 g   Sodium: 58.7 mg

Rich Fudgy Brownies
Better than regular brownies—moist and delicious!

8 squares	unsweetened chocolate	8 squares
1 C	olive oil	250 mL
4	eggs, or equivalent egg substitute	4
2 C	sugar	500 mL
1 C	black beans, cooked or canned and drained, and pureed	250 mL
1 C	flour	250 mL
1 t	baking powder	5 mL
2 T	instant coffee powder	30 mL
1 C	pecans, chopped	250 mL

Melt the chocolate with the oil in a small saucepan over low heat. Set aside. Beat the eggs one at a time. Put the sugar into the bowl of an electric mixer. Add the chocolate mixture and beat until well combined. Beat in the bean puree, flour, baking powder, and instant coffee powder. Fold in the nuts with a spatula. Pour and scrape the batter into a 9 × 13 inch (23 × 33 cm) pan coated with non-stick cooking spray. Smooth the top and bake in a 350°F (175°C) oven for 45 minutes. Cool completely in the pan before cutting into bars. *Yield: 16 brownies*

Calories per brownie: 333	Cholesterol: 0 mg
Total fat: 22.9 g	Fiber: 3.63 g
Saturated fat: 5.80 g	Sodium: 51.9 mg

Peanut Butter Granola Patties
Carob makes a healthy substitute for chocolate. If you can't find it in the supermarket, try a health food store.

1 C	peanut butter	250 mL
1/3 C	corn syrup	90 mL
1/4 C	carob powder	60 mL
1 C	raisins	250 mL
1 1/2 C	low fat granola	375 mL

In a medium-sized bowl, combine the peanut butter and corn syrup, mixing with a wooden spoon. Mix in the carob powder, then fold in the raisins and granola. It will make a fairly stiff dough. Roll into balls and flatten each one into a patty. Refrigerate between layers of waxed paper. *Yield: 54 patties*

Calories per patty: 51
Total fat: 2.6 g
Saturated fat: 0.52 g

Cholesterol: 0 mg
Fiber: 0.52 g
Sodium: 27.4 mg

Granola Squares
Keep these on hand for people who get the munchies in the afternoon.

2 C	oats, rolled	500 mL
½ C	pecans, coarsely chopped	125 mL
½ C	raisins	125 mL
1 t	cinnamon	5 mL
1 T	olive oil	15 mL
¼ C	molasses	60 mL
2 T	apple juice	30 mL
1	banana, ripe, mashed	1
1	egg or equivalent egg substitute, beaten	1

Combine the oats, pecans, raisins, and cinnamon in a medium-sized bowl. In another bowl, combine the olive oil, molasses, and apple juice and pour over dry mixture. Blend in the mashed banana and then the egg. Press the batter into 9-inch (23 cm) square baking dish greased with olive oil. Bake for 20 to 25 minutes in a 350°F (175°C) oven. Cool slightly and cut into 1½-inch squares. *Yield: 25 squares*

Calories per square: 68
Total fat: 2.5 g
Saturated fat: 0.30 g

Cholesterol: 0 mg
Fiber: 0.85 g
Sodium: 7.1 mg

No-Bake Granola Balls

Your friends and family will never suspect these treats act as laxatives.

1¼ C	oats, rolled	310 mL
½ C	almond pieces or chopped almonds	125 mL
1	egg, or equivalent egg substitute, lightly beaten	1
2 T	molasses	30 mL
½ C	peanut butter	125 mL
¼ C	oat bran	60 mL
2 T	dry milk powder	30 mL
½ t	cinnamon	2 mL
½ C	apricots, dried, chopped	125 mL
2 T	raisins	30 mL

Toast the oats, stirring frequently, in a heavy frying pan for 5 to 7 minutes, or until they are dry and crisp. Don't let them burn. Then, using the same pan, toast the almonds. Set aside.

Combine the lightly beaten egg, molasses, and peanut butter in a saucepan over low heat. Stir with a wooden spoon until the ingredients are well combined. Turn off the heat and transfer to a mixing bowl. Using an electric mixer at a low speed, add the toasted oats, oat bran, milk powder, cinnamon, apricots, and raisins. Roll into balls. Roll the balls in the toasted almonds to cover.
Yield: 28 balls

Calories per granola ball: 73
Total fat: 3.9 g
Saturated fat: 0.58 g

Cholesterol: 0.2 mg
Fiber: 0.96 g
Sodium: 33.1 mg

Pumpkin Cookies
It's amazing how delicious "health foods" can be!

1	egg or equivalent egg substitute	1
1 C	pumpkin, mashed	250 mL
¼ C	olive oil	60 mL
2 T	vanilla	30 mL
⅓ C	corn syrup	90 mL
1 C	whole wheat pastry flour	250 mL
¼ C	oat bran	60 mL
2 T	dry milk powder	30 mL
½ t	baking soda	2 mL
1 t	cinnamon	5 mL
¼ t	nutmeg	1 mL
¼ t	cloves, ground	1 mL
1½ C	oats, rolled	375 mL
½ C	raisins	125 mL
1 C	apricots, dried and chopped	250 mL

Combine egg, pumpkin, oil, vanilla, and corn syrup in a food processor, blender, or mixing bowl. Beat until smooth and creamy. In a medium-sized bowl, combine flour, oat bran, milk powder, baking soda, cinnamon, nutmeg, cloves, and oats. Add to the pumpkin mixture and mix briefly. Fold in the raisins and chopped apricots. Drop by teaspoonfuls on cookie sheets coated with non-stick cooking spray. Bake for 15 minutes or until firm and golden brown. Cool on a wire rack. *Yield: 56 cookies*

Calories per cookie: 44
Total fat: 1.2 g
Saturated fat: 0.17 g

Cholesterol: 0.1 mg
Fiber: 0.84 g
Sodium: 17.0 mg

Pumpkin Oat Bran Squares

Pumpkin is a naturally laxative food. Using canned pumpkin off the shelf makes this a quick treat.

1½ C	flour	375 mL
½ C	oats, uncooked (not instant or quick cooking)	125 mL
¼ C	oat bran	60 mL
2 t	baking powder	10 mL
1 t	cinnamon	5 mL
½ t	mace	2 mL
⅛ t	cloves	1 mL
2	egg whites	2
1 C	canned pumpkin	250 mL
½ C	pecans, chopped	125 mL
½ C	molasses	125 mL
¾ C	orange juice	190 mL
¼ C	canola oil	60 mL

In a bowl, mix together the flour, oats, oat bran, baking powder, and spices. In another bowl, beat the egg whites slightly and then add the remaining ingredients. Mix well. Pour the wet mixture over the dry and stir gently, just enough to moisten. Spoon into a 9-inch (23 cm) square baking pan coated with non-stick cooking spray oil. Bake at 375°F (190°C) for 25 minutes or so. Cool. Cut into squares. *Yield: 16 squares*

Calories per square: 143	Cholesterol: 0 mg
Total fat: 6.2 g	Fiber: 1.31 g
Saturated fat: 0.47 g	Sodium: 60.1 mg

Pumpkin Pie Squares
Fast and easy and great for people who pack lunches.

1 C	white flour	250 mL
½ C	oatmeal	125 mL
⅓ C	dark corn syrup	90 mL
¼ C	margarine or butter	60 mL
1½ C (12 oz)	evaporated milk	375 mL
1 can (15 oz)	pumpkin	1 can (420 g)
½ C	light corn syrup	125 mL
1 t	cinnamon	5 mL
	salt, to taste	
½ t	ginger	2 mL
2	eggs or equivalent egg substitute	2
¼ t	cloves or nutmeg	1 mL

Mix the flour, oatmeal, corn syrup, and margarine (or butter) in an electric mixer on low speed until crumbly. Press into ungreased 9″ × 13″ (23 × 33 cm) pan. Bake at 350°F (175°C) for 15 minutes. Combine remaining ingredients for the filling and pour over the crust. Bake at 350°F (175°C) for 25 minutes. Cut into squares.
Yield: 12 servings

Calories: 212
Total fat: 6.6 g
Saturated fat: 2.19 g

Cholesterol: 9.0 mg
Fiber: 2.13 g
Sodium: 72 mg

Apple Snacks
Quick cookies with lots of laxative appeal.

4	medium apples, cored and chopped	4
4 t	cinnamon	20 mL
1 T	dark corn syrup	15 mL
1 T	lemon juice	15 mL
1	egg or equivalent egg substitute	1
¼ C	oat bran cereal	60 mL
¼ C	oatmeal	60 mL
½ C	powdered nonfat milk	125 mL

Sprinkle the apples with cinnamon, and steam or microwave until tender. Liquefy in a blender. Combine the other ingredients; add the apple mixture. Stir. Drop by teaspoonfuls onto a cookie sheet coated with non-stick cooking spray. Bake in a 350°F (175°C) oven for 20 minutes. *Yield: 2 dozen cookies*

Calories per cookie: 34	Cholesterol: 0.5 mg
Total fat: 0.2 g	Fiber: 0.74 g
Saturated fat: 0.04 g	Sodium: 19.7 mg

Chewy Oat and Nut Treats
Good to make ahead and keep on hand.

¼ C	olive oil	60 mL
¼ C	corn syrup	60 mL
1	egg, or equivalent egg substitute	1
1 t	vanilla extract	5 mL
⅓ C	whole wheat pastry flour	90 mL
2 T	wheat germ	30 mL
½ t	cinnamon	2 mL
½ C	oats, rolled	125 mL
½ C	pecans, chopped	125 mL

Mix together all the ingredients except the nuts, using an electric mixer or food processor. Spoon the batter into a 9-inch (23 cm) square baking pan coated with non-stick cooking spray. Sprinkle nuts over the batter. Bake for 20 to 25 minutes in a preheated 350°F (175°C) oven, or until a toothpick inserted in center comes out clean. Cool slightly, then cut into squares. *Yield: 25 squares*

Calories for square: 149
Total fat: 3.8 g
Saturated fat: 0.44 g

Cholesterol: 0 mg
Fiber: 0.49 g
Sodium: 7.5 mg

No-Bake Grape-Nuts–Fig Squares
A tasty, crunchy snack that both children and adults will love!

½ C	molasses	125 mL
½ C	peanut butter	125 mL
2 T	olive oil	30 mL
½ C	figs, chopped	125 mL
½ C	dry milk powder	125 mL
2½ C	Grape-Nuts cereal	625 mL
1 T	grated orange rind	15 mL

Blend the molasses, peanut butter, and olive oil. Stir the chopped figs. Add the dry milk, Grape-Nuts, and orange rind, and mix well. Press firmly into a 9-inch (23 cm) square pan. Cool for at least one hour. Cut into squares. Keep refrigerated or frozen. *Yield: 25 squares*

Calories: 115
Total fat: 3.8 g
Saturated fat: 0.61 g

Cholesterol: 0.5 mg
Fiber: 2.15 g
Sodium: 109.0 mg

Prune Bars

Your friends will beg you for the recipe for this one.

1 C	prunes, chopped	250 mL
1 C	tart apples, unpeeled and chopped	250 mL
¼ C	dry sherry	60 mL
6 T	margarine or butter	125 mL
½ C	light brown sugar	125 mL
¼ C	molasses	60 mL
1	egg, or equivalent egg substitute, lightly beaten	1
1 t	vanilla	5 mL
½ C	flour	125 mL
¼ C	bran	60 mL
½ t	baking powder	2 mL
	salt, to taste	
1 t	cinnamon	5 mL
¼ t	allspice	1 mL
¼ t	nutmeg	1 mL
½ C	pecans, chopped	125 mL

Marinate the prunes and apples in the sherry for two hours. Cream the margarine (or butter), sugar, and molasses and then beat in the egg and vanilla. In a separate bowl, mix together the flour, bran, baking powder, salt, cinnamon, allspice, and nutmeg. Add the dry ingredients to the creamed mixture, blending well. Stir in the fruit mixture, and add the nuts. Mix until well combined. Spoon into an 8-inch (23 cm) square pan coated with non-stick cooking spray and bake at 350°F (175°C) for 35 minutes, or until lightly browned. When cool, cut into 2–3-inch squares. *Yield: 8 servings*

Calories per bar: 253
Total fat: 13.1 g
Saturated fat: 3.68 g

Cholesterol: 0 mg
Fiber: 3.68 g
Sodium: 144.5 mg

Date and Pecan Roll
Sinfully sweet and good for parties.

| ½ lb | pitted dates | .25 kg |
| 1 C | pecans | 250 mL |

Combine the dates and pecans in a food processor and chop. Use your hands to form the mixture into a one-inch (2.5 cm) roll. Cover with plastic wrap and refrigerate for several hours. Cut into slices.
Yield: 2 dozen slices

Calories per slice: 45
Total fat: 3.1 g
Saturated fat: 0.24 g

Cholesterol: 0 mg
Fiber: 0.80 g
Sodium: 0 mg

Stuffed Figs and Dates
Figs and dates are both natural laxative foods. Stuffed with walnut halves, they're fancy finger foods.

figs
pitted dates
shelled walnut halves (be sure to have
as many as figs and dates)

Cut out the center of each fig and place a walnut half inside. Cut open the dates and do the same.

Calories per stuffed fig: 64
Total fat: 1.8 g
Saturated fat: 0.18 g

Cholesterol: 0 mg
Fiber: 2.24 g
Sodium: 2.3 mg

Calories per stuffed date: 39
Total fat: 1.6 g
Saturated fat: 0.14 g

Cholesterol: 0 mg
Fiber: 0.84 g
Sodium: 0.3 mg

Apricot-Pecan Nuggets

Apricots have so many outstanding qualities: vitamins, beta-carotene, and laxative power.

¼ C	olive oil	60 mL
¼ C	corn syrup	60 mL
1	egg or equivalent egg substitute	1
1 t	vanilla	5 mL
1 C	canned pumpkin	250 mL
1 C	whole wheat pastry flour	250 mL
½ C	wheat germ	125 mL
½ C	oats, rolled	125 mL
1 t	baking soda	5 mL
1 t	cinnamon	5 mL
½ t	ginger	2 mL
½ t	nutmeg	2 mL
¾ C	apricots, dried and chopped	190 mL
½ C	pecans	125 mL

Mix together the egg, vanilla, olive oil, and corn syrup. Add the pumpkin, and blend to incorporate. In another bowl, combine the flour, wheat germ, rolled oats, baking soda, cinnamon, ginger, and nutmeg. Add the egg mixture and combine. Drop by the teaspoonfuls onto a cookie sheet coated with non-stick spray. Bake for 12–15 minutes in 350°F (175°C) oven. *Yield: 4 dozen small cookies*

Calories per cookie: 42
Total fat: 2.1 g
Saturated fat: 0.24 g

Cholesterol: 0 mg
Fiber: 0.84 g
Sodium: 27.6 mg

Sarah's Favorite Apricot Patties

Store a roll of these in the freezer. The patties slice easily even when frozen.

½	orange, seeded and peeled	½
	rind of ½ orange	
1½ C	apricots, dried	375 mL
¼ C	light corn syrup	60 mL
1 C	pecans, blender-chopped	250 mL
½ C	confectioners' sugar, sifted (optional)	125 mL

Blender-chop the orange, rind, and apricots. Spoon into a saucepan, add corn syrup, and cook about 30 minutes, stirring frequently. Cool. Add pecans to the cooled mixture and mix well. Shape into a long roll. Wrap in waxed paper and store in the freezer. Cut into thin slices and coat with confectioners' sugar just before serving. Make the full recipe and slice patties off as you want them. *Yield: about 36 patties*

Calories per patty: 36
Total fat: 2.0 g
Saturated fat: 0.16 g

Cholesterol: 0 mg
Fiber: 0.64 g
Sodium: 1.5 mg

Chapter 3: Soups

Hungarian Bean Soup

A traditional Hungarian soup. Like many traditional favorites, it is very high in laxative potential.

2	small onions, chopped	2
2 T	olive oil	30 mL
1	medium carrot, diced	1
2–3	large garlic cloves, minced	2–3
¼ t	ground black pepper	1 mL
1½ t	sweet Hungarian paprika	7 mL
3 T	white flour	45 mL
3 C	low-salt chicken stock	750 mL
2 C	navy beans, cooked or canned, drained	500 mL
¼ C	nonfat yogurt	60 mL
1 T	cider vinegar	15 mL
2 T	parsley, chopped	30 mL

Sauté the onion in the oil until the onion is translucent. Add the carrot and garlic and continue to sauté for a few minutes. Mix in the pepper and paprika. Sprinkle the flour into the vegetables, and stir; cook for a few more minutes. Add the chicken broth, and heat and stir until the mixture is thickened and the carrots are soft. Add the beans, stirring constantly. Remove the soup from the heat; whisk in the yogurt and then the vinegar. Gently reheat the soup for about 10 minutes, stirring constantly. Add parsley just before serving. *Yield: 4 servings*

Calories per serving: 387
Total fat: 11.1 g
Saturated fat: 1.71 g

Cholesterol: 3.8 mg
Fiber: 11.3 g
Sodium: 505 mg

Senate Bean Soup

This is called Senate Bean Soup because it has long been served in the U.S. Senate.

1 lb	dry beans, such as great northern, marrow, or peas	450 g
4.5 qt	water	4.5 L
2 t	liquid hickory smoke	10 mL
2	bay leaves	2
¼ t	white pepper	1 mL
2	medium-sized onions, finely chopped	2
2	carrots, finely chopped	2
2	celery stalks, finely chopped	2
2	garlic cloves, minced	2
1 C	mashed potatoes	250 mL

Cover the beans with cold water and soak overnight. The next day, drain off the soaking water. In a soup pot, combine the soaked beans, water, liquid smoke, bay leaves, and white pepper. Bring to a boil, turn down the heat and simmer until the beans are tender, about 2 to 2½ hours. Stir in the chopped vegetables and mashed potatoes. Cook for an additional 30 minutes. Remove the bay leaves. The soup can be served as is, or pureed in a food mill, blender, or food processor. *Yield: 12 cups*

Calories per serving: 136
Total fat: 0.5 g
Saturated fat: 0.07 g

Cholesterol: 0 mg
Fiber: 4.22 g
Sodium: 13.2 mg

Minestrone Soup

Don't let the long list of ingredients put you off this soup. It's easy to make, freezes well, and is hearty enough to stand alone as a meal.

2 T	olive oil	30 mL
1	large onion, chopped finely	1
2	cloves of garlic	2
2	medium carrots, diced	2
2	stalks celery, diced	2
¼ C	parsley, minced	60 mL
1 t	dry basil	5 mL
¼ C	dried sage	60 mL
	salt and pepper, to taste	
⅓ C	tomato sauce	90 mL
1 C	lima beans, cooked or canned, drained	250 mL
2 C	kidney beans, cooked or canned, drained	500 mL
6 C	low-salt cooking stock	1.5 L
2 C	cabbage, chopped	500 mL
¼ C	cornmeal	60 mL
	Parmesan cheese as garnish (optional)	

In a heavy saucepan, heat the olive oil over moderate heat. Sauté the onions, garlic, carrots, celery, parsley, and seasonings for 5 minutes, stirring frequently. Add the tomato sauce, stir well, and remove from heat. Puree about one half the kidney beans in a food processor or blender and add to the sautéed vegetables. Reserve the remaining beans.

Return the puree to the saucepan. Add the chicken stock. Bring to a boil over high heat. Stir in the cabbage. Lower the heat, simmer, covered, for 30 minutes, stirring occasionally. When the cabbage is cooked, add the reserved kidney beans and the lima beans. Season to taste. Pour the cornmeal into the soup in a thin stream, slowly, and stir continuously to prevent lumping. Cover and simmer 15 minutes more. *Yield: 8 servings*

Calories per serving: 179
Total fat: 6.9 g
Saturated fat: 1.29 g

Cholesterol: 3.8 mg
Fiber: 4.75 g
Sodium: 565 mg

Garbanzo Bean Soup

A wonderful, hearty soup for cold winter nights. A meal in itself.

3 T	olive oil	45 mL
3	garlic cloves, minced	3
2	leeks, carefully washed, thinly sliced	2
1	tomato, chopped	1
1 T	tomato paste	15 mL
½ t	rosemary	2 mL
2 C	chickpeas, cooked or canned, drained	500 mL
2 T	basil, fresh, minced or 1 T (15 mL) dried	30 mL
2 T	parsley, fresh, minced or 1 T (15 mL) dried	30 mL
6 C	chicken stock	1.5 L
½ C	orzo, rice-shaped macaroni	125 mL

Heat the olive oil in a large pot. Stir in the garlic and leeks and sauté, stirring frequently, until garlic is golden brown. Add the tomato paste and rosemary. Stir in the chickpeas, basil, parsley, and stock. Remove a cup of the soup and puree; add it back into the rest of the soup. Bring to rapid boil. Add the orzo and cook for 7 minutes, until the orzo is soft. *Yield: 6 servings*

Calories per serving: 226
Total fat: 11.9 g
Saturated fat: 2.02 g
Cholesterol: 5 mg
Fiber: 3.86 g
Sodium: 665 mg

Mediterranean Lima Bean Soup
Really easy. Just get it started and the flavors blend.

1 T	olive oil	15 mL
2	medium-sized onions, minced	2
2	cloves garlic	2
3 C	low-salt chicken broth	750 mL
2 T	corn syrup	30 mL
3 C	lima beans, cooked or canned and drained	750 mL
1 T	parsley	15 mL
	black pepper, to taste	
1 can (6 oz)	tomato paste	1 can (170 g)
¼ C	red wine vinegar	60 mL
1 t	oregano	5 mL
1 t	basil	5 mL
1 t	cilantro (coriander leaf) (optional)	5 mL
	salt and pepper, to taste (optional)	

Heat the oil in a large saucepan. Cook the onions and garlic until the onions are wilted. Add remaining ingredients. Cover and simmer for one hour. *Yield: 8 servings*

Calories per serving: 142
Total fat: 3.6 g
Saturated fat: 0.68 g
Cholesterol: 1.9 mg
Fiber: 3.30 g
Sodium: 256 mg

Quick Lentil-Barley Soup

If your family is not familiar with lentils, making a soup is a great introduction.

1	small onion, chopped	1
¼ C	olive oil	60 mL
9 C	water	2.3 L
12 oz	tomato paste	340 g
½ t	celery seed	2 mL
½ C	dry lentils	125 mL
⅓ C	whole barley	90 mL
¼ t	black pepper	1 mL
⅛ t	rosemary	1 mL
¾ t	basil	3 mL

In a large soup pot, sauté the onion in oil until soft, stirring with a wooden spoon. Add the remaining ingredients. Cover and cook gently for about 45 minutes, stirring occasionally. *Yield: 12 servings*

Calories per serving: 149	Cholesterol: 0 mg
Total fat: 7.4 g	Fiber: 2.90 g
Saturated fat: 1.0 g	Sodium: 35.5 mg

Yellow Pea Soup

You won't miss the ham in this traditional soup. Edith likes it with air-popped popcorn as a garnish.

2 C	dried yellow peas	500 mL
2 qt	chicken broth	2 L
1	small onion, sliced	1
1	clove garlic	1
¼ C	olive oil	60 mL
	salt and freshly ground pepper, to taste	
1 t	marjoram	5 mL
	salt and pepper, to taste (optional)	

Cook the peas and broth, simmering for about 2 hours. Puree the mixture in a blender or food processor. Sauté the onion, garlic, and olive oil until the onion is soft and golden. Puree this in a blender with a little of the soup. Combine the puree with the rest of the pea soup mixture and add salt, pepper, and marjoram. Heat to boiling. If desired, serve with garlic croutons and minced parsley. This soup freezes beautifully. *Yield: 8 servings*

Calories per serving: 163   Cholesterol: 5.0 mg
Total fat: 11.1 g   Fiber: 5.59 g
Saturated fat: 1.97 g   Sodium: 980 mg

Split Pea Soup

Hickory liquid smoke is a great substitute for the ham flavor cooks traditionally got by adding a ham bone.

1 lb	green split peas	450 g
1	stalk celery, diced	1
2	small carrots, diced	2
2	medium carrots, diced	2
8 C	water	2 L
1	bay leaf	1
½ t	thyme	2 mL
¼ t	white or black pepper	1 mL
1 t	hickory liquid smoke (optional)	1 mL
2 T	sherry (optional)	30 mL
1 C	skim milk	250 mL

Wash and pick out any discolored peas and combine with the vegetables in a soup pot. Add the water and the seasonings. Simmer until the peas are soft, about 2 hours. Remove the bay leaf. In a food mill or blender, puree the soup 2 cups (500 mL) at a time. If you like your soup lumpy, do not blend it all. Stir in the sherry, milk, and any additional water needed for a thinner consistency. Serve hot. *Yield: 10 servings*

Calories per serving: 69   Cholesterol: 0.4 mg
Total fat: 0.4 g   Fiber: 5.15 g
Saturated fat: 0.09 g   Sodium: 293.6 mg

Asparagus Soup

This soup rivals those served in the world's best restaurants, but is low in calories because potatoes, not heavy cream, thicken it.

1 T	olive oil	15 mL
1 lb	fresh asparagus, ends trimmed or 1 lb frozen asparagus	450 g
2	potatoes, finely chopped	2
3½ C	low-salt chicken broth	625 mL
2 t	lemon juice	10 mL
	white pepper and salt, to taste	
1 t	basil	5 mL
2 T	chives	30 mL

Combine the ingredients in a saucepan. Simmer ingredients 20 minutes, or until the potatoes and asparagus are tender, stirring occasionally. In a blender, puree mixture, a little at a time. Return it to a saucepan, stir in additional chicken broth to get the consistency you prefer, and simmer it 10 minutes more, stirring often. *Yield: 6 servings*

Calories per serving: 103
Total fat: 4.6 g
Saturated fat: 4.6 g

Cholesterol: 2.9 mg
Fiber: 2.29 g
Sodium: 381.2 mg

Sweet Potato Soup

Canned sweet potatoes work in this soup. Use the liquid in the can too. This soup may seem unusual at first but will come to be a favorite.

3 C	leeks or onions, thickly sliced	750 mL
3	carrots, cut into chunks	3
3	ribs celery, sliced into large chunks	3
2 T	olive oil	30 mL
4 C	low-salt chicken broth	1 L
4 C	cooked sweet potatoes, mashed or pureed	1 L
	freshly ground pepper, to taste	
½ t	tarragon	2 mL

In a soup pot, sauté the onions, carrots, and celery in olive oil, stirring frequently until the onions are limp. Add the chicken broth, and cover. Simmer until the vegetables are tender. Add the sweet potatoes with their liquid to the remainder of the soup, and puree. Add the tarragon and pepper to taste. *Yield: 8 servings*

Calories per serving: 183
Total fat: 2.4 g
Saturated fat: 0.59 g

Cholesterol: 2.5 mg
Fiber: 4.79 g
Sodium: 439.1 mg

Pumpkin Soup

Canned pumpkin or leftover "Halloween" pumpkin work equally well in this recipe. You could also substitute leftover winter squash.

4 C	pureed, cooked pumpkin	1 L
3	garlic cloves	3
2	onions, chopped	2
¼ t	marjoram	1 mL
2	stalks celery, chopped	2
2	tomatoes, chopped (or 1 cup, 250 mL, chopped canned tomatoes)	2
5 C	low-salt chicken stock	1.25 L
⅓ C	dry white wine	90 mL
1 T	corn syrup	15 mL
1 t	cinnamon	5 mL
	salt and pepper, to taste	

Place all ingredients, except the pumpkin, in a large saucepan. Bring to a boil, decrease heat and simmer for 30 minutes, covered. Add the pumpkin, stir with a whisk to combine, and simmer 5 minutes longer before serving. *Yield: 6 servings*

Calories per serving: 123
Total fat: 4.2 g
Saturated fat: 0.87 g

Cholesterol: 4.2 mg
Fiber: 8.08 g
Sodium: 558.9 mg

Squash Soup

Winter squash is loaded with nutrition, and this soup is smooth and delicious.

2 C	butternut squash, cooked and pureed	500 mL
3 C	chopped onion	750 mL
2 T	olive oil	30 mL
¼ t	nutmeg	1 mL
¼ t	cinnamon	1 mL
¼ t	dried thyme	1 mL
¼ t	ginger	1 mL
1	medium carrot, diced	1
2	celery stalks, chopped	2
1½ C	water	375 mL
1 C	pear juice	250 mL
1 C	orange juice	250 mL
	salt and pepper, to taste	

Sauté the chopped onion in the oil with the nutmeg, cinnamon, thyme, and ginger until the onion is soft. Add the diced carrot, celery, and water. Cover and simmer until the carrots are tender. Puree and return to the pot. Add the squash and juices; mix well. Gently reheat. Add salt and pepper to taste. *Yield: 8 servings*

Calories per serving: 113
Total fat: 4.0 g
Saturated fat: 0.59 g
Cholesterol: 0 mg
Fiber: 3.47 g
Sodium: 15.5 mg

Mushroom-Barley Soup

Very low in calories, it makes a great first-course soup.

1 T	margarine or butter	15 mL
1 T	safflower oil	15 mL
1	small onion, chopped fine	1
4 C	low-salt chicken stock	1 L
½ lb	fresh mushrooms, diced	225 g
¼ t	onion powder	1 mL
1	bay leaf	1
2 T	parsley, chopped	30 mL
¼ t	white pepper	1 mL
3 T	barley	45 mL
2 T	cornstarch	30 mL
1 C	skim milk	250 mL
¼ C	sherry (not cooking sherry)	60 mL
	salt, to taste (optional)	

Melt the margarine (or butter) in a soup pot; add the oil and onion and sauté for about 5 minutes. Add the chicken stock, mushrooms, onion powder, bay leaf, parsley, white pepper, and barley; cook over low heat for 45 minutes, stirring occasionally. In a small bowl, mix the cornstarch and milk, stirring with a wire whisk until smooth. Add to the soup pot. Reduce the heat and cook gently for 2 to 3 minutes until thickened, stirring constantly; remove the bay leaf. Before serving, stir in the sherry. *Yield: 8 servings*

Calories per serving: 108
Total fat: 5.7 g
Saturated fat: 1.02 g

Cholesterol: 3.0 mg
Fiber: 1.22 g
Sodium: 339.0 mg

Cream of Broccoli Soup

Broccoli is a wonderful source of beta-carotene and a natural laxative as well.

10 oz	frozen chopped broccoli*	300 g
¾ C	water	190 mL
2 T	olive oil	30 mL
1	small onion, diced	1
5 T	flour	75 mL
2 C	skim milk	500 mL
dash	allspice or	dash
2 T	sherry (not cooking sherry)	30 mL
	salt and pepper, to taste (optional)	

Cook the broccoli in the water, covered, for 4 or 5 minutes. Meanwhile, heat the olive oil in a soup pot, add the onion and sauté for 5 minutes. Sprinkle flour over the onions, stir, and cook over low heat for a minute or so. Add the broccoli and its cooking water; stir. Add the milk. Simmer but do not boil. Stir in the sherry or allspice. Season with salt and pepper. Cook gently a few minutes more. Serve warm or cold. *Yield: 6 servings*

Calories per serving: 120   Cholesterol: 1.3 mg
Total fat: 4.8 g   Fiber: 2.38 g
Saturated fat: 0.72 g   Sodium: 57.3 mg

*You can substitute 2 cups (500 mL) of fresh broccoli. Frozen broccoli and cauliflower with red peppers makes a colorful variation.

Cucumber-Yogurt Soup

This traditional Middle Eastern soup uses yogurt in a delicious way. For the most laxative version, use yogurt with acidophilus cultures.

4 C	cucumber, peeled, seeded, coarsely chopped	1 L
½ C	green onion, coarsely chopped (about 3), including green tops	125 mL
2 T	dill, chopped fresh	30 mL
¼ C	lemon juice, freshly squeezed	60 mL
1 C	chicken broth	250 mL
4 C	nonfat yogurt	1 L
	salt	
	white pepper, freshly ground	
	fresh radish slices for garnish	
	chopped fresh dill for garnish	

Combine cucumber, onion, dill, lemon juice, and chicken broth in a food processor or blender, and puree. Add yogurt and blend until fairly smooth. Season to taste with salt and pepper. To serve hot, heat in saucepan over low heat. Do not boil. *Yield: 6 servings*

Calories per serving: 108
Total fat: 1.0 g
Saturated fat: 0.23 g

Cholesterol: 0.8 mg
Fiber: 2.80 g
Sodium: 210.9 mg

Summer Soup

Our friends Joanne and her husband, Francis, argued over who would get the last little bit of this soup.

2 C	corn niblets, frozen or canned	500 mL
4 C	tomato juice	1 L
1	cucumber, peeled, cubed (seeded if the seeds are large)	1
2	Florida avocados, ripe, peeled, pitted, cubed	2
¼ C	lime or lemon juice	60 mL
1	large garlic clove, minced or pressed	1
dash	Tabasco sauce (liquid or hot pepper)	dash

Cook the corn in boiling water until just tender and drain well. Combine with the rest of the ingredients. Chill for one to two hours or until very cold. *Yield: 8 servings*

Calories per serving: 140   Cholesterol: 0 mg
Total fat: 8.2 g   Fiber: 4.97 g
Saturated fat: 1.31 g   Sodium: 581.2 mg

Quick Mexican Corn and Chicken Soup

With chicken, this is a one-dish meal.

1 T	olive oil	15 mL
1	medium-sized onion, minced	1
1	green or red pepper	1
3 C	corn niblets	750 mL
2 T	lemon juice	30 mL
2 T	dry sherry	30 mL
3 C	low-salt chicken broth	750 mL
	black pepper, to taste	
dash or 2	pepper sauce (Tabasco)	dash or 2
2 t	mustard	10 mL
⅛ t	nutmeg	.5 mL
2	boneless chicken breasts, cut into long strips (optional)	2

Heat the oil in a large saucepan. Sauté the onion till browned but not burned. Stir in corn and liquid, lemon juice, sherry, chicken broth, and all other ingredients. Bring to boil. Add chicken, if desired. Cover and simmer over low heat 15 minutes. Serve immediately or cover, chill, and serve cold. *Yield: 8 servings*

Calories per serving: 95	Cholesterol: 1.9 mg
Total fat: 4.0 g	Fiber: 3.82 g
Saturated fat: 0.73 g	Sodium: 243 mg

Corn Chowder
The secret to this tasty corn chowder is browning the onion.

2 T	olive oil	30 mL
1	medium onion, finely chopped	1
2	medium potatoes, peeled and cut into cubes	2
2 C	skim milk	500 mL
10 oz	frozen corn*	300 g
	salt and pepper, to taste (optional)	

Put the olive oil in a skillet over medium heat. Cook the onion until the pieces are browned. Mix onions, potato cubes, and milk in a saucepan. Simmer over medium heat for 20 minutes, but do not boil. Add the corn, salt, and pepper. Simmer for another 5 minutes. *Yield: 4 servings*

Calories per serving: 219	Cholesterol: 2.0 mg
Total fat: 7.7 g	Fiber: 5.18 g
Saturated fat: 1.18 g	Sodium: 265.8 mg

*If you like a thicker corn chowder, substitute a can of cream-style corn.

Potato-Leek Soup

You can use onions in place of the leeks. If you serve this soup cold, call it vichyssoise.

2 T	olive oil	30 mL
4	medium leeks	4
2 lb	potatoes (about 6 medium)	900 g
2 C	water	500 mL
¾ C	skim milk	190 mL
	white pepper and salt, to taste	

Put the olive oil into a soup pot. Thinly slice the white part of the leeks. Cook the leeks gently in oil for 10 minutes or so, until they are soft. Meanwhile, peel and dice the potatoes and add them to the soup pot with the leeks. Add the water, cover, and simmer until the potatoes are tender, about 30 minutes. Remove some of the potatoes to a bowl, depending on how chunky you like your soup. (The chunkier you like it, the more you should remove.) Put the remainder of the soup through a sieve, or mash it with a potato masher. Add the milk and the reserved potatoes. Correct the seasonings. Heat over low heat, but be careful not to let the soup boil. *Yield: 6 servings*

Calories per serving: 191
Total fat: 4.7 g
Saturated fat: 0.66 g

Cholesterol: 0.5 mg
Fiber: 3.42 g
Sodium: 26.9 mg

Georgia Soup

A fantastic and smooth treat.

¼ C	olive oil	60 mL
½ C	yellow onion, chopped	125 mL
½ C	celery, chopped	125 mL
6 C	yams, peeled and sliced	1.5 L
2 quarts	low-salt chicken stock	2 L
1¼ C	peanut butter, smooth	310 mL
	salt and pepper, to taste	
	chopped roasted peanuts for garnish (optional)	

Heat the olive oil in a saucepan over medium heat. Add the onion, celery, and yams and sauté until the onion and celery are soft but not browned, about 5 minutes. Add the stock and bring to a boil, then reduce the heat to low. Cover and simmer till yams are very tender, about 30 minutes. Remove from the heat and cool slightly. Puree in a food processor or blender. Add the peanut butter and puree until smooth. Add salt and pepper, to taste. Garnish with a few chopped roasted peanuts. This can be served hot or cold. When reheating, do not allow the soup to boil. *Yield: 16 servings*

Calories per serving: 281.5 Cholesterol: 2.5 mg
Total fat: 15.9 g Fiber: 3.48 g
Saturated fat: 2.72 g Sodium: 345 mg

Gazpacho
A traditional summer soup that is delicious when made with garden-fresh tomatoes.

1	medium cucumber, peeled, coarsely chopped	1
2	large, fresh tomatoes, chopped	2
1	medium onion, chopped	1
½	green pepper, seeded, chopped	½
1	garlic clove, chopped	1
4 slices	high-fiber bread, trimmed of crusts and crumbled	4 slices
1 C	water	250 mL
2 T	red wine vinegar	30 mL
1 T	olive oil	15 mL
¼ C	no-salt-added tomato paste	60 mL

Mix all the ingredients in a large bowl. Blend small amounts at a time in blender until it becomes a smooth puree. Chill several hours before serving. *Yield: 6 servings*

Calories per serving: 77 Cholesterol: 0 mg
Total fat: 2.9 g Fiber: 2.47 g
Saturated fat: 0.35 g Sodium: 11.8 mg

Beet Borscht
An almost instant soup with lots of taste.

1 can (8 oz)	beets	1 (can) 250 mL
1	small onion, quartered	1
1 C	potatoes, diced	250 mL
1 C	low-salt chicken stock	250 mL
1 T	lemon juice	15 mL
1 t	sugar	5 mL
1 C	more low-salt chicken stock	250 mL
	salt and pepper, to taste (optional)	
	optional: nonfat yogurt	

Blend the beets, onion, potatoes, and 1 C (250 mL) chicken stock in a blender or food processor until the vegetables are chopped. Pour mixture into a saucepan. Add the lemon juice, sugar, 1 C (250 mL) more chicken stock, salt, and pepper to taste. Simmer 10 minutes to blend flavors. Serve hot or cold with yogurt on top if desired. *Yield: 4 servings*

Calories per serving: 75	Cholesterol: 2.5 mg
Total fat: 2.2 g	Fiber: 2.07 g
Saturated fat: 0.53 g	Sodium: 439.5 mg

Prune Soup
This elegant soup can be served either warm or chilled. Some of our friends serve it for dessert but it is also an excellent first course in place of fruit cocktail.

about 40	pitted prunes, dried	about 40
1 qt	prune juice	1 L
2	cinnamon sticks	2
about 6	whole cloves	about 6
2 T	lemon juice, freshly squeezed	30 mL
½ C	toasted almonds (optional)	125 mL
1 T	ground cardamom, or to taste	15 mL

Combine the prunes, prune juice, cinnamon, and cloves in large saucepan over medium-high heat and bring to boil. Simmer, uncovered, until the prunes are plump and very tender, about 15 minutes. Cool slightly and discard the spices. Puree in a food processor or blender a few cups at a time until smooth. Stir in the lemon juice. Serve cold or hot. It is traditional to garnish this with chilled whipped topping flavored with a little ground cardamom. *Yield: 6 servings*

Calories per serving: 330	Cholesterol: 0 mg
Total fat: 6.3 g	Fiber: 7.20 g
Saturated fat: 0.62 g	Sodium: 100.3 mg

Scandinavian Fruit Soup

A delicious soup—the recipe has been handed down through generations.

1½ C	prunes, dried, pitted	375 mL
1½ C	apricots, dried	375 mL
3	apples, cored, diced	3
½ C	corn syrup	125 mL
1½ qt	water or fruit juice and water	1.5 L
1	stick of cinnamon	1
2 T	cornstarch mixed with a little cold water	30 mL

Cook all the ingredients except the cornstarch until tender. Remove the cinnamon stick and puree a cup of the mixture at a time in a blender or food processor. Return the soup to the saucepan and add the cornstarch–water combination. Cook and stir until it looks clear. Chill. Serve very cold. *Yield: 6 servings*

Calories per serving: 285	Cholesterol: 0 mg
Total fat: 0.3 g	Fiber: 8.0 g
Saturated fat: 0.04 g	Sodium: 18.3 mg

Cold Cranberry Soup
So easy and so good!

2 C	cranberries, fresh	500 mL
1 C	corn syrup	250 mL
1 T	tapioca (sago)	15 mL
¼ stick	cinnamon	¼ stick
2	lemon slices	2
2 C	water	500 mL

Put all the ingredients in a small saucepan. Bring to a boil. Boil for 10 minutes. Remove the cinnamon and 1 lemon slice. Puree the rest of the mixture in a blender. Chill and serve garnished with your favorite topping. *Yield: 4 servings*

Calories per serving: 280
Total fat: 0.1 g
Saturated fat: 0.01 g

Cholesterol: 0 mg
Fiber: 2.23 g
Sodium: 55.3 mg

Chapter 4: Salads

French Bean Salad

The type of salad you would expect to be served in a very fancy French restaurant.

1 can (15.5 oz)	butter beans	1 can (445 mL)
3	medium tomatoes, chopped	3
1	mild onion, peeled, chopped	1
½ C	almonds, slivered	125 mL
2	stalks celery, chopped	2
1	clove garlic, finely chopped	1
⅓ C	pitted ripe olives, halved	90 mL
3 T	parsley, chopped	45 mL
	salt and black pepper, to taste	

Dressing

¼ C	tomato sauce	60 mL
2 T	lemon juice	30 mL
1 T	Worcestershire sauce	15 mL
1 T	olive oil	15 mL

Combine the beans with the vegetables, almonds, and seasonings. In a separate bowl, whisk together the dressing ingredients; pour over the bean mixture. Serve chilled. *Yield: 6 servings*

Calories per serving: 159
Total fat: 9.2 g
Saturated fat: 1.01 g
Cholesterol: 0 mg
Fiber: 4.26 g
Sodium: 158.2 mg

Three Bean Salad

To reduce the sodium content of canned beans, put them in a colander and rinse well under running cold water.

1 C	kidney beans (canned or cooked)	250 mL
1 C	white kidney beans (canned or cooked)	250 mL
1 C	chickpeas (canned or cooked)	250 mL
¾ C	onion, finely chopped	190 mL
2 T	parsley, finely chopped	30 mL
1	green pepper, chopped finely	1
⅓ C	olive oil	90 mL
⅓ C	cider vinegar	90 mL
¼ C	corn syrup	60 mL
	salt and pepper, to taste	

Mix all the ingredients; refrigerate several hours or overnight to blend the flavors. *Yield: 6 servings*

Calories per serving: 281
Total fat: 13.2 g
Saturated fat: 1.78 g
Cholesterol: 0 mg
Fiber: 4.03 g
Sodium: 420.7 mg

One Bean Salad

Like Three Bean Salad, but even easier. Try it—you'll like it.

1 can (15 oz)	pinto beans, rinsed, drained	1 can (430 mL)
1	stalk celery	1
2 T	green onion, thinly sliced	30 mL
3 T	vinegar	45 mL
1½ T	molasses	22 mL
1 T	olive oil	15 mL
1 t	Dijon-style mustard	5 mL
	salt and pepper, to taste (optional)	
	lettuce leaves	

Combine the beans, celery, and green onion. For the dressing, combine the vinegar, molasses, oil, mustard, salt, and pepper. Mix well. Pour the dressing over the bean mixture; stir to coat. Cover and chill for 4 to 24 hours, stirring occasionally. Serve over lettuce leaves. *Yield: 4 servings*

Calories: 141
Total fat: 3.8 g
Saturated fat: 0.53 g

Cholesterol: 0 mg
Fiber: 7.37 g
Sodium: 28.8 mg

Garbanzo Salad
Make this the day before, to blend the flavors.

2 T	onion, minced	30 mL
1	clove garlic, crushed	1
¼ t	basil	1 mL
½ t	oregano	2 mL
2 T	olive oil	30 mL
1 T	wine vinegar	15 mL
	salt and pepper, to taste (optional)	
½ t	Dijon mustard	2 mL
1 can (15 oz)	chickpeas, drained	1 can (430 mL)
1 T	nonfat mayonnaise	15 mL
2 T	parsley, fresh, minced	30 mL

Combine all the ingredients except the mayonnaise and parsley. Marinate overnight in the refrigerator. Just before serving add the mayonnaise and parsley. *Yield: 8 servings*

Calories per serving: 88
Total fat: 3.9 g
Saturated fat: 0.51 g

Cholesterol: 0 mg
Fiber: 1.69 g
Sodium: 157.6 mg

Lentil Salad

Served on a lettuce leaf, this salad is elegant and tasty.

2 C	water	500 mL
	salt (optional)	
1 C	lentils	250 mL
2 T	olive oil	30 mL
1½ T	vinegar	22 mL
½ C	scallions or onions, chopped	125 mL
½ C	parsley, fresh, chopped	125 mL
	salt and pepper, to taste	
	lettuce	

Combine the water and salt, if used, in large saucepan. Add the lentils and boil gently for 45 minutes or until tender. Cool. Combine oil, vinegar, scallions, and parsley, and add to cooled lentils. Season to taste. Refrigerate. Serve each portion on a single lettuce leaf. *Yield: 6 servings*

Calories per serving: 85	Cholesterol: 0 mg
Total fat: 4.7 g	Fiber: 1.67 g
Saturated fat: 0.63 g	Sodium: 2.8 mg

Coleslaw

Using nonfat mayonnaise in this recipe cuts back on the calories but not on the natural laxative power of coleslaw.

1 lb	small head of cabbage, shredded	450 g
1	carrot, grated	1
1	small onion, peeled, diced	1
½ C	nonfat mayonnaise dressing	125 mL
¼–½ t	celery seed	1–2 mL
1 T	light corn syrup	15 mL
1 T	cider vinegar	15 mL
	salt and pepper, to taste	
	(optional)	

Mix the cabbage, carrot, and onion in a large bowl. In a small bowl, combine the mayonnaise, celery seed, corn syrup, vinegar, salt, and pepper. Toss with the shredded vegetables. Refrigerate until ready to serve. This tastes better after aging for a few hours. *Yield: 7 servings*

Calories per serving: 51
Total fat: 0.2 g
Saturated fat: 0.02 g

Cholesterol: 0 mg
Fiber: 2.73 g
Sodium: 189.3 mg

Blueberry Salad

Blueberries are a natural laxative. In this recipe they team up with other natural laxatives, such as apples, nuts, and yogurt to make a surprisingly wonderful salad.

1 C	nonfat yogurt	250 mL
¼ C	wheat germ	60 mL
1 T	lemon juice	15 mL
½ C	blueberries	125 mL
¼ C	oats, rolled	60 mL
1 t	grated orange rind	5 mL
1½ T	honey	22 mL
2	apples, unpeeled, chopped	2
¼ C	nuts, chopped	60 mL

Mix together the yogurt, oats, wheat germ, orange rind, lemon juice, and honey. Add the apples and nuts to the yogurt mixture. Combine gently. Keep refrigerated until serving. *Yield: 6 servings*

Calories per serving: 120
Total fat: 3.8 g
Saturated fat: 0.38 g

Cholesterol: 0 mg
Fiber: 2.28 g
Sodium: 25.5 mg

Vegetable-Pineapple Gelatin Salad

This salad is worth the extra trouble. In many families it's a holiday favorite for anything from Fourth of July cookouts to the Thanksgiving dinner table.

2	carrots, grated	2
1 C	cabbage grated	250 mL
20 oz	crushed pineapple and juice from the can	600 g
small amount	water	small amount
2 env.	unflavored gelatin	2 env.
¼ C	sugar	60 mL
1 C	ice water	250 mL
2 T	lemon juice	30 mL
2 drops	yellow food coloring (optional)	2 drops

Combine the grated carrots and cabbage in a bowl. Add drained pineapple to the carrots and cabbage, reserving the juice. Combine the juice with enough water to make 2 cups (500 mL). Pour this liquid into a saucepan, and bring to a boil. Add the gelatin and sugar, and stir until dissolved. Stir in the ice water, lemon juice, and optional food coloring. To be sure the pieces do not sink to the bottom, chill this mixture until it is slightly thicker than an unbeaten egg white, about 45 minutes. Fold in the pineapple and grated vegetables and pour into the prepared mould. To be sure gelatin will unmould without sticking, spray the mould with non-stick cooking spray.

To unmould a gelatin salad, fill a large bowl with hot water. Immerse the mould in water to the rim for about 20 seconds. Remove the mould from the water and hold a serving plate over it. Using both hands, invert so that the serving plate is on the bottom. Still holding the mould and plate together, give the mould a little shake. When you feel the gelatin dropping onto the plate, lift off the mould. *Yield: 4 servings*

Calories per serving: 173	Cholesterol: 0 mg
Total fat: 0.2 g	Fiber: 2.89 g
Saturated fat: 0.02 g	Sodium: 22.3 mg

Seasonal Fruit Gelatin Salad

Use fruit that is fresh and in season when you make this gelatin salad.

2 env.	unflavored gelatin	2 env.
¼ C	cold water	60 mL
½ C	boiling water	125 mL
⅓ C	sugar	90 mL
1 C	apple, orange, or cranberry juice	250 mL
2 drops	food coloring (optional)	2 drops
2 T	lemon juice	30 mL
2 C	small pieces of fruit, such as fresh or frozen cantaloupe balls, seedless grapes, apples, or canned pineapple chunks	500 mL

Stir the gelatin into the cold water to soften it. Add the boiling water and stir until the gelatin dissolves. Add the sugar, juice, and food coloring, if desired; stir. To be sure that the pieces of fruit will be evenly distributed, chill the mixture until it is as thick as unbeaten egg white, about 30 to 45 minutes. Fold in the fruit and spoon the whole mixture into a lightly oiled or sprayed mould.

To unmould a gelatin salad, fill a large bowl with hot water. Immerse the mould in water to the rim for about 20 seconds. Remove the mould from the water and hold a plate over it. Using both hands, invert so that the serving plate is on the bottom. Still holding the mould and plate together, give the mould a little shake. When you feel the gelatin dropping onto the plate, lift off the mould. *Yield: 4 servings*

Calories per serving 131	Cholesterol: 0 mg
Total fat: 0.3 g	Fiber: 0.72 g
Saturated fat: 0.02 g	Sodium: 13.4 mg

Jellied Salad
You can cut down on the calories by using sugar-free gelatins.

1 pkg. (3 oz)	orange gelatin	1 pkg. (90 mL)
1 pkg. (3 oz)	lemon gelatin	1 pkg. (90 mL)
2 C	boiling water	500 mL
1 C	cold water	250 mL
1 can (20 oz)	crushed pineapple	1 can (600 g)
1 can (11 oz)	mandarin oranges, drained	1 can (310 g)
½ C	sherry	125 mL

Dissolve the gelatin in boiling water and add cold water. Let cool, then add the remaining ingredients. Pour into a mould and refrigerate. Stir mixture as it begins to jell so the fruit will not settle to the bottom. *Yield: 6 servings*

Calories per serving: 184
Total fat: 0.2 g
Saturated fat: 0.01 g

Cholesterol: 0 mg
Fiber: 1.19 g
Sodium: 39.4 mg

Cranberry-Pear Salad
So easy. So colorful. So healthy.

1 C	nonfat yogurt	250 mL
1 C	whole-berry cranberry sauce	250 mL
¼ C	sugar	60 mL
16	pear halves	16

Combine the yogurt, cranberry sauce, and sugar. Cover and freeze overnight in a small bowl. When serving, scoop out frozen mixture with a spoon or melon baller. Fill each pear half with scoops of frozen mixture. *Yield: 16 servings*

Calories per serving: 93
Total fat: 0.4 g
Saturated fat: 0.02 g

Cholesterol: 0 mg
Fiber: 2.56 g
Sodium: 14.1 mg

Waldorf Salad
A classic treat, much healthier with yogurt in place of mayonnaise.

2	apples, large, firm, ripe, cored, unpeeled, diced	2
2 t	lemon juice	10 mL
2 T	nonfat yogurt	30 mL
2 T	walnuts, coarsely chopped	30 mL
	lettuce leaves	

Toss the apples in a bowl with the lemon juice. Just before serving, add the yogurt; toss to coat the apples; mix in the walnuts. Serve on lettuce leaves. *Yield: 4 servings*

Calories per serving: 67
Total fat: 2.1 g
Saturated fat: 0.21 g

Cholesterol: 0 mg
Fiber: 1.96 g
Sodium: 9.9 mg

Astoria Salad
The new nonfat mayonnaise products can make low-calorie cooking a snap.

2 C	apples, diced, unpeeled	500 mL
1 C	bananas, sliced	250 mL
1 C	celery, diced	250 mL
2 T	nonfat mayonnaise	30 mL
1 C	orange or grapefruit sections	250 mL
¾ C	peanuts, chopped, roasted	190 mL

Combine all ingredients and toss lightly. Refrigerate until serving. *Yield: 6 servings*

Calories per serving: 207
Total fat: 9.0 g
Saturated fat: 1.62 g

Cholesterol: 0 mg
Fiber: 5.29 g
Sodium: 285.0 mg

Chapter 5: Side Dishes

Barbecued Corn on the Cob

You can't imagine the great taste of this corn on the cob until you've tried it.

2 T	olive oil	30 mL
1 C	ketchup	250 mL
2 T	vinegar	30 mL
2 t	dry mustard	10 mL
¼ t	ginger	1 mL
¼ t	onion powder	1 mL
	salt and pepper, to taste	
4	ears of corn, fresh or frozen	4

To make the barbecue sauce, combine all the ingredients except the corn in a small bowl. Lay each ear of corn on a 12-inch (30 cm) square of aluminum foil. Brush the sauce on each ear of corn, spreading the sauce over the entire surface. Seal the foil but don't wrap it tightly around the corn, allowing room for steam. Arrange the ears on a cookie sheet, seam-side up. Roast in a 400°F (200°C) oven for 45 minutes. *Yield: 4 servings*

Calories per serving: 213
Total fat: 8.3 g
Saturated fat: 1.09 g

Cholesterol: 0 mg
Fiber: 8.02 g
Sodium: 460 mg

Stir-Fried Broccoli

This quick side dish takes 5 minutes to cook and will boost the laxative power of a meal substantially.

2 T	olive oil	30 mL
1	head broccoli, separated into flowerets, stalks cut into 1-inch (2.5 cm) rounds	1
8	cloves garlic, minced	8
8	mushrooms, sliced	8
1 T	wheat bran	15 mL

Heat the oil in a large skillet. Add the broccoli and garlic. Stir over medium heat for 3 minutes or until the garlic is browned. Stir in the mushrooms and wheat bran and stir-fry for another 2 minutes. Serve over pasta. *Yield: 8 servings*

Calories per serving: 49
Total fat: 3.5 g
Saturated fat: 0.47 g

Cholesterol: 0 mg
Fiber: 1.77 g
Sodium: 10.6 mg

Stuffed Acorn Squash

Adding the stuffing to the acorn squash makes it even more delicious.

8	large pitted prunes, cut into small pieces	8
½ C	Port wine	125 mL
2 (12–16 oz)	acorn squash, halved, seeded	2 (350–450 g)
¼ C	olive oil	60 mL
2 T	onions, chopped	30 mL
4	small apples, cut into ½ inch (1 cm) cubes	4
¼ C	almond slivers	60 mL

Soak the prunes in wine until plump. Place the squash cut-side down in a baking dish with about ½ inch (1 cm) water. Bake in a 350°F (175°C) oven until tender, about 20 minutes. Heat the oil and onion in a medium-sized skillet until the onions are tender. Add the apples and sauté. Remove the squash, turn the halves over and prick them with a fork. Drain the prunes and spoon 1 T (15 mL) of drained wine over each squash half. Mix the nuts and prunes with the apple mixture. Scoop into the squash centers. Spoon the remaining wine over filling. Cover and return to the oven for 20 minutes. *Yield: 4 servings*

Calories per serving: 407   Cholesterol: 0 mg
Total fat: 19.6 g   Fiber: 12.87 g
Saturated fat: 2.62 g   Sodium: 5.0 mg

Curried Bulghur with Cashews and Raisins
Never tried bulghur? You'll be pleasantly surprised.

1 T	olive oil	15 mL
1	medium onion, chopped	1
2 T	raisins	30 mL
1 t	curry powder	5 mL
⅓ C	cashews	90 mL
1 C	bulghur wheat	250 mL
2 C	chicken stock	500 mL
	salt, to taste	

Heat the olive oil in a large skillet. Add the onion and sauté for 2 minutes. Stir in the raisins, curry powder, and cashews, then add the bulghur wheat, chicken stock, and salt. Mix well. Bring to a boil, cover, reduce heat, and cook over very low heat for 15 to 20 minutes. Use a fork to fluff. Serve immediately. *Yield: 4 servings*

Calories per serving: 194   Cholesterol: 2.5 mg
Total fat: 11.0 g   Fiber: 2.63 g
Saturated fat: 2.0 g   Sodium: 589.7 mg

Vegetable Curry

Feel free to substitute broccoli for the cauliflower. If you use yogurt, buy the kind with acidophilus.

4	medium potatoes, quartered, unpeeled, scrubbed	4
1 T	olive oil	15 mL
24 oz (3 C)	cauliflower flowerets	750 mL
1 t	ginger	5 mL
1 t	curry powder	5 mL
	salt and pepper, to taste	
½ t	turmeric	2 mL
¼ C	water	60 mL
10 oz	peas, frozen	300 g
1 C	yogurt, plain, nonfat (optional)	250 mL
	chutney (optional)	

Cook the potatoes in water in a covered pot for 15 minutes, or until done. Heat the oil in a large skillet and sauté the cauliflower and seasonings over medium heat for about 30 seconds. Stir in the seasonings and the water. Mix thoroughly to coat the cauliflower with the spice mixture. Cover and cook over low heat, about 5 minutes, until the cauliflower is tender. Stir in the peas and remove from heat. When the potatoes are tender, drain them and add to the skillet. Stir thoroughly, coating the vegetables with spices. Cook over medium heat, just long enough to cook peas, 2–3 minutes. Serve with yogurt and chutney. *Yield: 4 servings*

Calories per serving: 256
Total fat: 3.9 g
Saturated fat: 0.55 g

Cholesterol: 0 mg
Fiber: 8.32 g
Sodium: 91.3 mg

Queen Cauliflower

A special presentation.

1	cauliflower	1
2 T	olive oil	15 mL
2 T	wheat germ	15 mL
2 T	bread crumbs from high-fiber bread	15 mL

Trim the leaves and stem of the cauliflower but leave it whole and put it into a cooking pot with a tight-fitting lid. Add 2 cups (500 mL) of water and cover tightly. Cook over high heat until the water begins to boil; turn down the heat and allow the cauliflower to cook in the steam until fork-tender, about 15 to 20 minutes. Drain cauliflower in a colander. Stir the oil, wheat germ, and bread crumbs together. Press the mixture onto the top of the cauliflower, like a crown. (This can be done ahead of time and refrigerated.) Just before serving, set the cauliflower in a pie plate and bake in a 350°F (175°C) oven for 5 to 10 minutes. *Yield: 8 servings*

Calories per serving: 51
Total fat: 3.7 g
Saturated fat: 0.49 g

Cholesterol: 0 mg
Fiber: 1.28 g
Sodium: 7.5 mg

Sweet Potato Casserole
Not just for Thanksgiving.

3 C	sweet potatoes, cooked, mashed (about 2 large sweet potatoes, peeled)	750 mL
¼ C	molasses	60 mL
2 T	olive oil	30 mL
4	eggs, or equivalent egg substitute, beaten	4
¼ C	light rum	60 mL
¼ t	cinnamon	1 mL
	salt, to taste	

Combine the sweet potatoes with the rest of the ingredients. Beat well by hand or with electric mixer. Fold into a 2-quart baking dish sprayed with non-stick cooking spray. Bake for 45 to 50 minutes. When the casserole is done a knife inserted in the center should come out clean. The casserole will be firm and golden. *Yield: 8 servings*

Calories per serving: 202
Total fat: 3.6 g
Saturated fat: 0.50 g

Cholesterol: 0 mg
Fiber: 2.15 g
Sodium: 140.2 mg

Sweet Potatoes and Bananas

This is so sweet and delicious. It almost seems like a dessert. Great for people who hate to eat their veggies.

2 C	sweet potatoes, mashed	500 mL
1 T	sugar	15 mL
½ t	vanilla extract	2 mL
⅓ C	wheat bran	90 mL
2	bananas, mashed	2
⅔ C	sliced almonds	180 mL

In a bowl combine the sweet potatoes, sugar, and vanilla. Add the wheat bran and bananas. Put in baking dish coated with non-stick cooking spray. Sprinkle with the almond slices. Bake at 350°F (175°C) for 15 minutes. *Yield: 4 servings*

Calories per serving: 266
Total fat: 11.6 g
Saturated fat: 1.18 g

Cholesterol: 0 mg
Fiber: 5.50 g
Sodium: 15.2 mg

Sweet Potatoes and Cranberries

Don't save this recipe for Thanksgiving. You'll want to have it much more often.

6	sweet potatoes, cooked, peeled, and halved, or canned	6
½ t	cinnamon	2 mL
2 C	whole cranberry sauce	500 mL

Place sweet potatoes cut-side down in a greased, shallow casserole. Sprinkle with cinnamon. Spread cranberry sauce all over them. Bake in a 350°F (175°C) oven for 20 minutes. *Yield: 8 servings*

Calories per serving: 193
Total fat: 0.2 g
Saturated fat: 0.03 g

Cholesterol: 0 mg
Fiber: 2.79 g
Sodium: 28.3 mg

Cranberry Relish
A traditional favorite.

1	orange, unpeeled	1
1	apple, unpeeled	1
2 C	cranberries, washed	500 mL
½ C	celery, washed, sliced	125 mL
½ C	walnuts	125 mL
	sugar, honey, or Aspartame	

Cut the orange and apple into quarters and remove the seeds. Blender-chop the cranberries, celery, and walnuts. Mix well and add the sweetener. Store in the refrigerator. *Yield: 8 servings*

Calories per serving: 71
Total fat: 4.0 g
Saturated fat: 0.37 g

Cholesterol: 0 mg
Fiber: 2.38 g
Sodium: 7.5 mg

Cooked Cranberry-Orange Relish
Soft and sweet.

¼ C	water	60 mL
¼ C	orange juice	60 mL
½ C	sugar	125 mL
½ lb (2 C)	cranberries	500 mL
1 T	orange rind, grated	15 mL

Stir the water, orange juice, and sugar together in a 3- or 4-quart saucepan until the sugar is dissolved. Add the cranberries, bring to a boil, and cook for 3 to 5 minutes, until the skins of the berries begin to pop and the berries are tender. Stir in the orange rind. Transfer the mixture to a serving bowl, let cool, and then chill for at least an hour or two before serving. *Yield: 30 spoonfuls*

Calories per serving: 16
Total fat: 0 g
Saturated fat: 0 g

Cholesterol: 0 mg
Fiber: 0.27 g
Sodium: 0.1 mg

Uncooked Cranberry-Orange Relish

Make this relish as coarse or as fine as you like by deciding how much to grind it.

2 C	cranberries	500 mL
1	orange, quartered	1
1 C	sugar, more to taste	250 mL

Put the berries and orange through a grinder. Stir in the sugar. Chill or freeze. *Yield: 30 servings*

Calories per serving: 30	Cholesterol: 0 mg
Total fat: 0 g	Fiber: 0.39 g
Saturated fat: 0 g	Sodium: 0.1 mg

Corn Relish

A natural laxative side-kick for barbecues.

⅔ C	cider vinegar	180 mL
2 T	cornstarch	30 mL
1 t	pickling spice	5 mL
¼ t	cinnamon	1 mL
⅓ C	sugar	90 mL
10 oz	frozen corn	300 g
½	red or green pepper, finely diced	½
	salt and pepper, to taste	
	(optional)	

Combine the vinegar, cornstarch, pickling spice, cinnamon, and sugar in a saucepan. Simmer for 15 minutes, stirring occasionally. Meanwhile, cook the frozen corn as directed on the label; drain. Mix with the chopped pepper. Pour the sauce over the corn and peppers. If desired, strain and discard the spices before using the sauce. Refrigerate overnight to blend the flavors. *Yield: 12 servings*

Calories per servings: 41	Cholesterol: 0 mg
Total fat: 0.2 g	Fiber: 0.93 g
Saturated fat: 0.03 g	Sodium: 49.6 mg

Date Relish
Dates are one of the best natural laxatives, and this is a delicious way to include them with a meal.

1	onion, thinly sliced	1
20	pitted dates, sliced lengthwise	20
3 T	cider vinegar	45 mL
1 t	sugar	5 mL
	salt, to taste (optional)	

Place the onion slices in a bowl and cover with boiling water. After 15 minutes, drain the water. Combine onion slices with dates, vinegar, sugar, and salt, if desired. *Yield: 4 servings*

Calories per serving: 130   Cholesterol: 0 mg
Total fat: 0.1 g   Fiber: 3.88 g
Saturated fat: 0.01 g   Sodium: 0.5 mg

Fun Fiesta Pea Pods with Raspberries
Everyone who has seen and tried this comments on its eye-appeal as well as the fabulous taste.

½ lb	snow pea pods, washed, tips removed	240 g
1 T	vinegar	15 mL
2 T	olive oil	30 mL
	salt and pepper, to taste	
¾ C	raspberries	190 mL

Bring a saucepan of water to boil and add the peas. Cook for 3 minutes at full boil. Drain well in a colander, then toss in a serving bowl with vinegar, oil, salt, and pepper until well coated. Stir in the raspberries gently, being careful not to mash them. Serve warm. *Yield: 5 servings*

Calories per serving: 57   Cholesterol: 0 mg
Total fat: 5.5 g   Fiber: 0.90 g
Saturated fat: 0.73 g   Sodium: 0 mg

Baked Beans
An American classic.

1 lb	dry white beans	450 g
2 T	dry mustard	30 mL
⅓ C	dark molasses	90 mL
1	onion, chopped	1
2 T	vinegar	30 mL
1	pork chop, small, trimmed (optional)	1

Wash the beans, place them in a bowl with water to cover, and soak them overnight. The next morning discard the soaking water, mix the beans with all the other ingredients in a bean pot or casserole, and add water to cover. Cover the casserole and place it in a 300°F (150°C) oven. Bake for several hours or all day. Check beans from time to time, adding water if necessary. This dish is done when the beans are soft and the liquid has evaporated. *Yield: 8 servings*

Calories per serving: 227   Cholesterol: 6.6 mg
Total fat: 1.9 g   Fiber: 4.99 g
Saturated fat: 0.37 g   Sodium: 13.2 mg

Cranberried Beans
A different way to serve baked beans and cranberries.

2 cans (16 oz)	baked beans, canned	2 cans (450 g)
1 can (16 oz)	whole cranberry sauce, canned	1 can (450 g)
1	small onion, grated	1
4 t	dry mustard	20 mL

Arrange a layer of beans, a layer of cranberries, and a sprinkling of onion and mustard in a 2-quart casserole dish. Repeat, ending with a layer of beans. Bake in a 350°F (175°C) oven for 30 minutes. *Yield: 8 servings*

Calories per serving: 218   Cholesterol: 0 mg
Total fat: 1.0 g   Fiber: 5.0 g
Saturated fat: 0.52 g   Sodium: 390 mg

Boston Baked Beans

*A New England Saturday-night favorite. Cook them all day
Saturday.*

1 lb	dried peas or great northern beans	500 g
3	medium whole onions, peeled	3
3	cloves	3
2 t	salt (optional)	10 mL
½ C	molasses	125 mL
½ C	brown sugar	125 mL
1 T	mustard	15 mL
1 t	black pepper	5 mL
2 T	vinegar	30 mL
1	small pork chop, trimmed of fat	1

Put the beans in a large saucepan, cover with cold water and soak
overnight. Bring to a boil. Boil for a few minutes. Remove from
the heat and let set for 1 hour. Bring to a boil again and add the
onion, then simmer for 30 minutes. Drain the beans and discard
the water.

Place 2 onions, each stuck with a clove, on the bottom of a 2-
quart (2-L) bean pot or casserole dish. Cover with beans. Combine
molasses, brown sugar, mustard, salt, and pepper to taste in small
mixing bowl. Pour this mixture over the beans and push the pork
chop so it is covered with the mixture, slightly below the surface.
Cover tightly and bake in the center of a 250°F (125°C) oven for
5 hours. *Yield: 8 servings*

Calories per serving: 236	Cholesterol: 6.6 mg
Total fat: 1.4 g	Fiber: 3.70 g
Saturated fat: 0.43 g	Sodium: 49 mg

Curried Lentils and Cashews

*Everyone who tastes this wants the recipe. A delightful
combination of flavors.*

8 oz	red lentils	240 g
1⅔ C	onions, coarsely chopped	330 mL
1 t	garlic, minced, in oil	5 mL
2 T	olive oil	30 mL
1 T	curry powder	15 mL
¼ t	ground cinnamon	1 mL
1 C	low-salt chicken stock	250 mL
1 (about 4½ C)	small to medium cauliflower flowerettes	1 (1.5 L)
3 oz	tomato paste, canned	85 g
½ C	cashews, unsalted, roasted salt, to taste	125 mL
½ C	plain nonfat yogurt	125 mL

Bring the lentils to a boil in plenty of water. Cover and cook until
soft, about 10 minutes. In a frying pan, sauté the onion and garlic
in hot oil until soft. Reduce the heat and add curry powder and
cinnamon. Add the cauliflower to the frying pan, then add the
chicken stock and tomato paste. Mix well. Cover and cook until
the cauliflower is soft. Drain the lentils, reserving the liquid, and
add the lentils to the cauliflower mixture. Thin the sauce by adding
liquid from the pot, if necessary. Stir in the cashews. Serve with
yogurt on the side. *Yield: 2 servings*

Calories: 602	Cholesterol: 2.5 mg
Total fat: 33.2 g	Fiber: 13.07 g
Saturated fat: 5.64 g	Sodium: 368 mg

Lentils and Chickpeas

2	onions, chopped	2
2 C	red lentils	500 mL
3¾ C	vegetable stock	940 mL
1 T	olive oil	15 mL
7	celery sticks, chopped	7
1 can (19 oz)	chickpeas, drained	1 can (550 g)
¼ C	dry white bread crumbs	60 mL
2 T	Parmesan cheese, grated	30 mL
	salt and pepper, to taste	
	(optional)	

Put 1 onion in a saucepan with the lentils, then add the stock. Bring to a boil. Reduce the heat, cover tightly, and cook gently for 25 minutes, until all the stock has been absorbed and the lentils are tender. Add salt and pepper. Spread half the lentil mixture in a baking dish coated with non-stick cooking spray. Heat the oil in a heavy-bottomed saucepan. Add the remaining onion and celery. Cover and cook over medium heat, stirring occasionally, for about 15 minutes, or until onions are softened.

Stir the chickpeas into the celery mixture, with a little seasoning. Cover and cook for 5 minutes. Spread the mixture over the lentil base, patting evenly with the back of a spoon. Top with the remaining lentils. Spread them out in an even layer. Mix the bread crumbs and Parmesan cheese. Sprinkle the mixture over the lentils and bake for 20 minutes, or until golden brown, crisp, and hot. *Yield: 6 servings*

Calories per serving: 243
Total fat: 6.5 g
Saturated fat: 1.42 g
Cholesterol: 4.7 mg
Fiber: 6.01 g
Sodium: 320 mg

Lima Beans and Pears

Both lima beans and pears are great laxatives. They team up wonderfully in this easy recipe.

1 can (16 oz)	large lima beans	1 can (465 mL)
1 can (16 oz)	pear halves, drained (reserve juice)	1 can (465 mL
⅓ C	brown sugar	90 mL

Layer beans and pears in a casserole dish coated with non-stick cooking spray; begin and end with beans. Pour on ½ cup (125 mL) pear juice and bake at 350°F (175°C) for 1–1½ hours, until lightly brown and syrupy. *Yield: 8 servings*

Calories per serving: 122
Total fat: 0.2 g
Saturated fat: 0.04 g
Cholesterol: 0 mg
Fiber: 2.87 g
Sodium: 7.8 mg

Lentils and Fruits

A casserole you'll be proud to serve. Fancy enough for company yet simple enough for an everyday side dish.

1 C	dried lentils, rinsed	250 mL
2 T	raisins	30 mL
1 t	garlic, minced	5 mL
1	small onion, peeled, chopped	1
1	tomato, large, peeled, seeded and chopped (or canned tomatoes, chopped)	1
1½ T	olive oil	22 mL
⅔ C	canned pineapple chunks	180 mL
½	medium-firm banana, peeled and sliced	½
1	apple, cored, diced	1
	salt and pepper, to taste (optional)	

Place the lentils in a saucepan with the raisins and cover with water. Over high heat, bring to a boil. Reduce the heat, simmer, and cook, covered, for 25 minutes. Drain. While the lentils and raisins are cooking, puree the garlic, onion, and tomato in a food processor or blender until smooth. Heat the oil in a skillet over high heat until hot, but not burning. Add the tomato puree and stir steadily for three minutes. Reduce the heat to a simmer. Add the pineapple, banana, apple, salt, and pepper. Cook for 5 minutes more. Add the lentil-raisin mixture to the puree-fruit mixture and simmer for 10 more minutes, stirring occasionally. *Yield: 6 servings*

Calories per serving: 173	Cholesterol: 0 mg
Total fat: 4.0 g	Fiber: 4.91 g
Saturated fat: 0.55 g	Sodium: 4.4 mg

Refried Beans

This Southwestern favorite is a natural laxative. Eat refried beans as a side dish or as a sandwich spread.

2 C	kidney beans, cooked or canned (about one 19 oz, or 550 g, can)	500 mL
1	onion, chopped	1
1	clove garlic, minced	1
2 T	olive oil	30 mL
1 t	chili powder	5 mL
½ C	tomato paste	125 mL
	salt and pepper, to taste	

Heat the oil in a large skillet and add the onion, garlic, and chili powder. Cook gently for a few minutes; turn off heat. Add the tomato sauce and a small amount of beans to the skillet. Mash with a potato masher. Continue to add beans and mash them in the skillet. Serve warm. *Yield: 8 servings*

Calories per serving: 189	Cholesterol: 0 mg
Total fat: 7.4 g	Fiber: 4.72 g
Saturated fat: 1.0 g	Sodium: 129 mg

Chickpeas and Green Peas

Both chickpeas and green peas are natural laxatives. This recipe combines them in a delicious way. If you use yogurt as a topping, buy the kind with acidophilus cultures.

2 T	olive oil	30 mL
1	garlic clove, crushed	1
1	onion, chopped	1
1 T	cumin seeds	15 mL
1 T	poppy seeds	15 mL
1½ t	dry mustard	7 mL
	salt and pepper, to taste	
1 pkg. (10 oz)	frozen peas	1 pkg. (300 mg)
1 can (14 oz)	chickpeas, drained	1 can (400 mg)
½ C	water	125 mL
	nonfat yogurt (optional)	

Heat the olive oil and sauté the garlic and onion with seasonings for 10 minutes. Add the peas and water. Bring to a boil, lower the heat, and simmer, uncovered, for 5 minutes. Stir in the chickpeas and cook until the liquid has evaporated. Be sure the peas have cooked completely. Serve immediately, topped with yogurt, if desired. *Yield: 4 servings*

Calories per serving: 228	Cholesterol: 0 mg
Total fat: 9.0 g	Fiber: 7.11 g
Saturated fat: 1.16 g	Sodium: 322.1 mg

Baked Pears

Fresh pears baked in juice make an easy side dish. And many people find pears one of the best natural laxatives.

4	medium pears, firm, ripe	4
¼ C	orange or lemon juice	60 mL

Wash the pears and slice off the tip of the stem end; core the pears. You may wish to cut decorative "V"-shaped wedges or scallops around the edges of the pears. Baste the pears with the juice. Place them cut-side up in a pie plate lined with foil for easy cleanup. Bake in a 350°F (175°C) oven for about 30 minutes. *Yield: 4 servings*

Calories per serving: 105   Cholesterol: 0 mg
Total fat: 0.7 g   Fiber: 4.83 g
Saturated fat: 0.04 g   Sodium: 0.1 mg

Cabbage with Apples
An inexpensive winter side dish. Keeps well in the refrigerator.

1	medium head of red or white cabbage	1
2	medium apples, unpeeled, sliced	2
1	medium onion, chopped	1
2 T	margarine or butter	30 mL
¼ C	vinegar	60 mL
2 T	sugar	30 mL
1 t	crushed caraway seeds	5 mL
2 T	water	30 mL

Shred the cabbage using a food processor, hand grater, or knife. Mix the apples and onion with the cabbage. Melt the margarine (or butter) in a large saucepan. Add the vegetables and stir for about 5 minutes. Add the remaining ingredients; cover the pot and cook gently for 35 minutes; add more water, if needed. Remove the cover and cook for 10 minutes more to boil down any excess liquid. *Yield: 8 servings*

Calories per serving: 71   Cholesterol: 0 mg
Total fat: 3.0 g   Fiber: 2.29 g
Saturated fat: 0.58 g   Sodium: 39.0 mg

Rice and Peas

Easy, yet looks like a gourmet recipe.

¼ C	olive oil	60 mL
½ C	celery, finely chopped	125 mL
1	medium onion	1
1 T	parsley, chopped finely	15 mL
1 C	brown rice	250 mL
4 C	low-salt chicken broth, heated	1 L
1 pkg. (10 oz)	frozen tiny peas	1 pkg. (310 mL)
⅓ C	Parmesan, freshly grated salt and pepper, to taste (optional)	90 mL

In a saucepan, sauté the celery and onion in olive oil until the vegetables become soft and brown on the edges. Stir frequently. Add the rice, and stir to coat thoroughly with oil, about 2 or 3 minutes. One ladleful at a time, add the hot chicken stock to the saucepan, stirring constantly. Simmer until the stock is absorbed and the rice is tender, about 20 minutes. Add the peas and combine well. Cook for 5 more minutes. Remove the pan from the heat and add the Parmesan cheese. Stir well. Allow it to stand for 4 or 5 minutes. Correct the seasonings. Serve immediately. *Yield: 8 servings*

Calories per serving: 142　　Cholesterol: 5.3 mg
Total fat: 10.1 g　　Fiber: 1.92 g
Saturated fat: 2.11 g　　Sodium: 264 mg

Chapter 6: Main Dishes

Chicken with Apples

Easy and tasty. You'll make this over and over again.

6	apples, unpeeled, cored, sliced	6
1	medium onion, cut into rings	1
3	chicken breasts, skinned, halved	3
½ C	dry sherry	125 mL
¼ C	lemon juice	60 mL
2 t	oregano	10 mL
½ t	rosemary	2 mL
¼ t	cinnamon	1 mL
3 T	nonfat yogurt	45 mL

Place the apple slices in a casserole dish and cover with onions. Top with the chicken. Pour sherry and lemon juice on top. Sprinkle the chicken with the herbs and cinnamon. Cover and bake for 45 minutes in 350°F (175°C) oven. Uncover and spoon the yogurt on the chicken. Bake, uncovered, 15 minutes more. *Yield: 6 servings*

Calories per serving: 212
Total fat: 2.9 g
Saturated fat: 0.74 g

Cholesterol: 44 mg
Fiber: 3.95 g
Sodium: 44.3 mg

Chicken Fajitas

Did you think fajitas were for restaurants only? This recipe makes them easy.

1 lb	chicken breast, boneless, skinless, cut in 1-inch (2.5 cm) strips	480 g
1	green pepper, sliced	1
1	onion, sliced	1
	juice of half a lime	
½ t	chili powder	2 mL
8	flour tortillas (6-inch, or 15 cm, size)	8
	guacamole (optional)	
	salsa (optional)	
	refried beans (optional)	
	salt and pepper, to taste (optional)	

Stir-fry the chicken and vegetables in a pan coated with non-stick cooking spray. Add the lime juice and chili powder. Warm the tortillas in microwave on high, about 50 seconds, or in non-stick skillet. Fill each tortilla with chicken mixture, guacamole, salsa, and refried beans.

Roll the tortilla with the filling inside to close. *Yield: 8 servings*

Calories per serving: 135	Cholesterol: 44.0 mg
Total fat: 3.0 g	Fiber: 1.24 g
Saturated fat: 0.76 g	Sodium: 69.3 mg

Whole Wheat Tortillas

Use these whole wheat tortillas for the chicken fajitas.

¼ C	bran	60 mL
1½ C	white flour	375 mL
1¼ C	whole wheat flour	310 mL
6 T	margarine (or butter)	90 mL
1 C	water	250 mL

Stir together the bran, flours, margarine (or butter), and water. Turn onto a floured board and knead until smooth. The dough will be stiffer than bread dough. Divide it into 16 equal balls for thin tortillas. Work each ball until smooth and pliable. Roll each as thinly as possible on a lightly floured board, adding more flour as needed.

Drop onto a very hot, ungreased griddle, cooking each until it is freckled on one side. Turn the tortilla and cook it on the second side. Keep the tortillas soft until serving by putting each one between the folds of a dish towel. *Yield: 16 tortillas*

Calories per tortilla: 110
Total fat: 4.5 g
Saturated fat: 0.78 g

Cholesterol: 0 mg
Fiber: 1.70 g
Sodium: 1.8 mg

Tex-Mex Guacamole for Fajitas

Great with corn tortilla chips, or use small pieces of fresh vegetables as dippers.

1	large Florida avocado, soft and ripe	1
1 T	onion, minced	15 mL
1 T	lemon juice	15 mL
¼ t	ground pepper	1 mL
dash	Tabasco sauce	dash
	salt and pepper, to taste	
1	large tomato, ripe	1

Cut the avocado in half, lengthwise. Discard the large pit and scoop the avocado into a bowl (save the skins to refill, if you like). Add the onion and seasonings; mash, using a fork, potato masher, or plastic blade of a food processor. Peel and dice the tomato and add it to the avocado. Serve immediately or chill before serving. *Yield: 8 servings*

Calories: 44
Total fat: 3.9 g
Saturated fat: 3.9 g

Cholesterol: 0 mg
Fiber: 0.89 g
Sodium: 5.2 mg

Baked Meatballs

Oatmeal boosts the laxative potential of meatballs. They are baked instead of fried to reduce the calories.

1 lb	extra lean ground beef	480 g
2	egg whites	2
1 T	dried parsley	15 mL
¾ C	oatmeal	190 mL
2 T	nonfat milk mixed with ½ C (125 mL) water	30 mL
	salt, to taste (optional)	
¼ t	ground pepper	1 mL
dash	nutmeg	dash

Mix all the ingredients together. Shape into 1½-inch balls. Arrange on two baking sheets coated with non-stick cooking spray. Bake for 12 minutes, or until done, in a 425°F (220°C) oven. *Yield: 6 servings*

Calories per serving: 166	Cholesterol: 48.2 mg
Total fat: 5.8 g	Fiber: 0.59 g
Saturated fat: 2.03 g	Sodium: 55.3 mg

Barley and Ground Beef

Barley adds fiber to this main dish.

½ lb	very lean ground beef	240 g
½ C	onion, chopped	125 mL
½ C	green pepper, chopped	125 mL
¼ C	celery, chopped	60 mL
	pepper, to taste	
2 t	sugar	10 mL
1 t	Worcestershire sauce	5 mL
½ C	chili sauce	125 mL
1 can (16 oz)	tomatoes, broken up	1 can (450 g)
1¾ C	uncooked barley	440 mL

Sauté the meat, onion, peppers, and celery in a non-stick frying pan. Drain the excess fat. Stir in remaining ingredients and bring to a boil. Reduce heat to simmer. Cover and cook about 1 hour (35 minutes for quick-cooking barley). *Yield: 6 servings*

Calories per serving: 297
Total fat: 3.4 g
Saturated fat: 1.09 g

Cholesterol: 24.0 mg
Fiber: 5.38 g
Sodium: 170.6 mg

Chili con Carne

A traditional favorite, this version is heavy on the beans and has less beef—a healthy choice.

1 lb	very lean ground beef	480 g
1 T	safflower oil	15 mL
1	green pepper, seeded, chopped	1
1	medium onion, finely chopped	1
2	cloves garlic, finely chopped	2
grind	fresh pepper	grind
1 t	oregano	5 mL
½ t	paprika	2 mL
1 t	cumin	5 mL
1 t	chili powder	5 mL
6 oz	low-salt tomato paste mixed with 2 cans (340 mL) of water	170 mL
3 C	kidney beans (cooked without salt)	750 mL

Cook the beef in the skillet over medium heat, stirring with a fork and breaking the meat into small chunks until no pink color is left. Drain off any fat. (You can put a double layer of paper towels on a dinner plate and use a slotted spoon to put the cooked meat on the towels.) In the same skillet, heat the oil over medium heat and sauté the onions, chopped pepper, and garlic for a few minutes or until tender, stirring frequently. Remove from heat and stir in seasonings. Add tomato paste and water, drained beef, and kidney beans. Bring to boil, lower heat, and simmer for about 1 hour. *Yield: 6 servings*

Calories per serving: 281 g
Total fat: 8.2 g
Saturated fat: 2.3 g

Cholesterol: 48.0 mg
Fiber: 4.69 g
Sodium: 494.7 mg

Beef and Prune Pie with Cobbler
A little extra trouble, but well worth it.

Filling

1 lb	lean round, cubed	450 g
1	large onion, peeled and sliced	1
4	large carrots, peeled and sliced	4
2	medium potatoes, peeled, thinly sliced	2
2 C	low-salt chicken stock	500 mL
	salt and pepper, to taste	
1 T	cornstarch	15 mL
2 T	margarine or butter	30 mL
1 C	pitted prunes cut in half	250 mL

Cobbler Topping

⅔ C	white flour	180 mL
⅓ C	wheat bran	90 mL
1 C	whole wheat flour	250 mL
1 T	baking powder	15 mL
pinch	dry mustard	pinch
	salt and pepper, to taste	
¼ C	margarine or butter	60 mL
2	egg whites, beaten	2
approx. ½ C	nonfat milk	approx. 125 mL

To make the filling: Arrange the beef, onion, carrots, potatoes, and seasonings in an ovenproof casserole dish. Pour the chicken stock over the top and cook in 350°F (175°C) oven for 1 hour. Moisten the cornstarch with a little cold water and stir it into the casserole. Cook for 10 minutes more. Raise the temperature to 400°F (200°C) and stir in the prunes.

To make the cobbler topping: Sift the flours with the baking powder, mustard, salt, and pepper. Cut in the margarine (or butter), then add the beaten egg whites and enough milk to form a stiff dough. Put the dough on a floured surface and roll to a thickness of approximately ¾ inch (2 cm). Use a biscuit cutter to stamp out circles of dough. Arrange the dough toppings on top of the Beef and Prune Pie. Brush the topping with milk. Bake until golden brown, about 30 minutes. *Yield: 6 servings*

Calories per serving: 401 Cholesterol: 50 mg
Total fat: 10.9 g Fiber: 6.51 g
Saturated fat: 2.99 g Sodium: 538.2 mg

Chili-Bean Meat Loaf

Adding beans to this meat loaf recipe doesn't change the flavor or consistency.

2 cans (1 lb)	red kidney beans	2 cans (450 g)
1 lb	super-lean ground beef	450 g
1	egg white	1
2	slices high-fiber bread, crumbled	2
½ C	oatmeal	125 mL
½ t	dry oregano	2 mL
1 T	dry basil	15 mL
1 T	Worcestershire sauce	15 mL
1 can	tomato paste	1 can
1 C	water	250 mL
	salt and cayenne pepper, to taste	

Drain the liquid from the canned kidney beans. Place the beans in a blender or food processor to puree. With clean hands, combine the beans, beef, egg white, bread crumbs, oatmeal, and seasonings. Press into a loaf pan. Combine tomato paste with water and pour over bean-beef mixture. Bake uncovered at 350°F (175°C) for one hour. *Yield: 8 servings*

Calories per serving: 278 Cholesterol: 36.5 mg
Total fat: 5.3 g Fiber: 4.51 g
Saturated fat: 1.67 g Sodium: 583.1 mg

Bean and Kielbasa Stew

Almost every ingredient in this stew is a natural laxative. The kielbasa adds a spicy flavor.

1 T	garlic, fresh, chopped	15 mL
1	large onion, sliced	1
¼ C	olive oil	60 mL
¼ lb	kielbasa or chorizo, low-fat, sliced	120 g
⅓ C	ketchup	90 mL
1 C	beef stock	250 mL
½ t	cayenne pepper (use less for a less spicy taste)	2 mL
1 can (15 oz)	pumpkin	1 can (450 g)
¼ C	parsley, diced	60 mL
1 C	lima beans	250 mL
1 C	chickpeas	250 mL
	salt and freshly ground pepper, to taste	

Sauté the garlic and onion in a large soup pot for about 8 minutes, stirring occasionally. At the same time, boil water in a separate saucepan. Drop the sliced sausage in the water, turn off the heat, and let it sit there. This removes any remaining fat. When the onions and garlic are soft, add the ketchup, beef stock, cayenne pepper, and pumpkin. Using a wire whisk, combine them. Add the chickpeas, lima beans, and drained sausage. Season to taste with salt and pepper. Simmer over low heat to combine flavors. *Yield: 6 servings*

Calories per serving: 227	Cholesterol: 4.0 mg
Total fat: 10.3 g	Fiber: 6.12 g
Saturated fat: 1.46 g	Sodium: 608 mg

Beef and Bean Stew

Kidney beans are a natural laxative addition to what is otherwise a traditional dish.

¾ lb	round steak, trimmed, cut in 1-inch (2.5 cm) cubes	350 g
1¾ C	kidney beans, canned	440 mL
1½ t	olive oil	7 mL
1 can (28 oz)	tomatoes, cut up	1 can (750 g)
¾ C	dry red wine	190 mL
1 t	sugar	5 mL
1	clove garlic, minced	1
	salt, to taste	
¼ t	thyme leaves	1 mL
2	bay leaves	2
3	potatoes, unpeeled, cubed	3
1	medium onion, cut in wedges	1
2	carrots, cut in chunks	2
	pepper, to taste	

Brown the meat in olive oil in a Dutch oven. Add the beans, tomato, wine, sugar, garlic, salt, thyme, and bay leaves to taste. Bring to boil; reduce heat. Cover and simmer for 1 hour, or until the meat is nearly tender. Add the potatoes, onions, and carrots. Cook 30 minutes more or until the meat and vegetables are tender. Before serving, remove the bay leaves. *Yield: 4 servings*

Calories per serving: 451
Total fat: 8.2 g
Saturated fat: 2.46 g
Cholesterol: 54.0 mg
Fiber: 8.32 g
Sodium: 448.6 mg

Curry Stuffed Squash

A one-dish meal with a healthy balance—a small amount of beef and a satisfying vegetable.

2	large acorn squash, split lengthwise in half, seeded	2
1 T	olive oil	15 mL
½ lb	very lean ground beef	240 g
4	chili peppers, chopped	4
½ t	curry powder	2 mL
	black pepper, to taste	
1	medium onion, minced	1
1	clove garlic	1
½ C	bread crumbs (use pieces of high-fiber bread)	125 mL
dash	ginger	dash

Bake the squash in a 350°F (175°C) oven, about 30 minutes. Heat the oil in a skillet. Add the meat and cook over low heat for 5 minutes, or until no pink color is left, stirring often. Add the remaining ingredients. Cook over medium heat 2 minutes, stirring continuously until blended well. Spoon the meat mixture into the squash cavities. Cover with foil and bake 10 minutes more, until the squash is tender. *Yield: 4 servings*

Calories per serving: 236 g
Total fat: 8.8 g
Saturated fat: 2.15 g

Cholesterol: 36.0 mg
Fiber: 7.2 g
Sodium: 29.9 mg

Bean Stroganoff

Pinto beans replace beef in this Stroganoff recipe. Yogurt increases the natural laxative power. (Sour cream is traditional.)

3 C	mushrooms, chopped	750 mL
2	medium onions, sliced	2
2 t	olive oil	10 mL
¼ C	flour	60 mL
¾ C	low-salt chicken stock	190 mL
¼ C	sherry	60 mL
4 t	Worcestershire sauce	20 mL
⅛ t	marjoram leaves	.5 mL
⅛ t	chili powder	.5 mL
⅛ t	thyme leaves	.5 mL
dash	nutmeg	dash
½ t	garlic powder	2 mL
3 C	pinto beans, cooked, drained	750 mL
1½ C	plain nonfat yogurt	375 mL
1 t	lemon juice, freshly squeezed	5 mL
	salt and pepper, to taste (optional)	

In a large skillet, sauté the mushrooms and onions in oil until tender. Mix the flour, chicken stock, sherry, Worcestershire sauce, and spices. Stir in the beans, heat over low heat, stirring frequently until beans are thoroughly cooked. Remove from heat and stir in yogurt and lemon juice. *Yield: 6 servings*

Calories per serving: 217
Total fat: 2.8 g
Saturated fat: 0.46 g

Cholesterol: 0.6 mg
Fiber: 10.94 g
Sodium: 177.8 mg

Couscous with Chickpeas

People who can't imagine themselves eating couscous or chickpeas will be surprised at how delicious this dish is. The zesty sauce is fabulous.

Couscous

2 T	olive oil	30 mL
1	medium onion, finely chopped	1
2 C	chicken stock, homemade or canned	500 mL
1 C	medium-grain quick-cooking couscous	250 mL
1 C	chickpeas, cooked or canned, drained, rinsed	250 mL
1½ C	leftover chicken, pork, or lamb diced into ½-inch (1 cm) cubes	375 mL

Zesty Sauce

⅓ C	olive oil	90 mL
4 t	paprika	20 mL
2 t	garlic, minced	10 mL
	salt, to taste	
⅛ t or more	cayenne pepper, to taste	.5 mL or more

To make the couscous: Sauté the onion in olive oil over medium-high heat in a medium saucepan until soft, about 3 or 4 minutes. Add the chicken stock and bring to a boil. Pour the couscous in a stream into the boiling liquid. Stir constantly. Boil for 2 minutes, remove from heat, stir in the chickpeas and leftover meat, if desired. Cover and allow to stand until the couscous is tender, about 10 to 20 minutes. Fluff the mixture with two forks. Serve with Zesty Sauce. *Yield: 6 servings*

To make the sauce: Mix all the sauce ingredients in a small bowl until thoroughly blended.

Calories per serving: 479
Total fat: 24.0 g
Saturated fat: 4.26 g
Cholesterol: 49.7 mg
Fiber: 1.99 g
Sodium: 376.3 mg

Beans and Broccoli

A hearty dish for a cold-winter dinner.

½ lb	white navy or great northern dried beans	250 g
	salt, to taste (optional)	
¼ t	dried thyme	1 mL
3 oz	ham, diced into small squares	90 g
1	onion, peeled, diced	1
2 T	olive oil	30 mL
2	cloves garlic, peeled, crushed, and finely chopped	2
good dash	cayenne pepper	good dash
½ lb	broccoli, washed, cut in small pieces	250 g
¼ C	water	60 mL

Wash the beans in cool water and remove and discard any pebbles or damaged beans. Combine the beans with 4 cups (1 L) cold water, salt, thyme, ham, and onions. Bring to a boil, cover and reduce heat, and gently boil for about 1½ hours, until beans are tender and most of the water has been absorbed. There should be just enough water so the beans are moist and juicy.

Heat the oil in a skillet, add the garlic, and sauté briefly. Add the broccoli (still wet from washing) and sauté for about 1 minute. Add the water. Cover and cook over medium heat for 10 minutes, until broccoli is soft. Just before serving, combine the beans and broccoli and reheat if necessary. Add a little olive oil to each serving, if desired. *Yield: 4 servings*

Calories per serving: 318
Total fat: 11.2 g
Saturated fat: 2.41 g

Cholesterol: 13.5 mg
Fiber: 9.44 g
Sodium: 289.8 mg

Louisiana Red Beans and Rice

A traditional dish that is packed with natural power.

1 lb	red kidney beans, cooked (reserve cooking broth)	480 g
3 T	olive oil	45 mL
2	large onions, chopped	2
3	cloves garlic, mashed	3
2	large green peppers, chopped	2
2	large stalks celery, sliced	2
2	bay leaves	2
½ t	thyme	2 mL
¼ t	cumin	1 mL
1 t	paprika	5 mL
½ C	tomatoes, peeled and chopped	125 mL
1 T	vinegar	15 mL
	hot pepper sauce, to taste	
	salt, to taste (optional)	
4 C	brown rice cooked	1 L

Heat the olive oil in a large saucepan and sauté onions, garlic, green peppers, and celery. Add the bay leaves, thyme, cumin, paprika, tomatoes, vinegar, and some bean broth. Simmer until the vegetables are tender. Add the beans with the remaining broth, hot pepper sauce, and salt shortly before serving. Boil, lower heat, and simmer about 5 minutes. Serve over steamed brown rice. *Yield: 8 servings*

Calories per serving: 174
Total fat: 5.7 g
Saturated fat: 0.79 g

Cholesterol: 0 mg
Fiber: 4.30 g
Sodium: 197 mg

Black Beans and Rice

If you use canned black beans, rinse them to reduce the sodium.

3 C	black beans, cooked	750 mL
1	clove garlic, minced	1
	salt and pepper, to taste (optional)	
4 C	brown rice, cooked	1 L
	salsa (optional)	

Serve the black beans mixed with the minced garlic over the cooked brown rice. If desired, top with salsa. *Yield: 8 servings*

Calories per serving: 180   Cholesterol: 0 mg
Total fat: 0.9 g   Fiber: 6.86 g
Saturated fat: 0.75 g   Sodium: 276.6 mg

Pintos and Prunes
A great fast meal that's high in natural laxative power.

2 C	pinto beans, cooked	500 mL
¼ C	olive oil	60 mL
1	large onion, chopped	1
1	clove garlic, mashed	1
2 C	tomatoes, peeled, chopped	500 mL
¾ C	prunes, pitted, chopped	190 mL
2 T	vinegar	30 mL
¼ C	apple juice	60 mL
⅛ t	cinnamon	.5 mL
dash	cloves	dash
dash	nutmeg	dash
2	bay leaves	2
	salt and pepper, to taste	
2 T	lemon juice	30 mL

Heat the olive oil in a large skillet or saucepan. Lightly brown the onion and garlic. Add all the ingredients except the beans and lemon juice and simmer for 20 to 30 minutes or until the onion and prunes are well cooked.

Combine the beans, lemon juice, and prune mixture. Serve over cooked brown rice. *Yield: 4 servings*

Calories per serving: 298   Cholesterol: 0 mg
Total fat: 7.6 g   Fiber: 14.65 g
Saturated fat: 1.06 g   Sodium: 198.2 mg

Bean and Tuna Salad

You'll like this better than plain tuna salad. The white beans pick up the tuna flavor but add lots of natural laxative power.

1 can (6½ oz)	solid white tuna, packed in water	1 can (182 g)
1 can (16 oz)	cannellini beans, drained, rinsed	1 can (450 g)
1	medium onion, finely chopped	1
1 T	parsley, chopped	15 mL
1½ t	oregano	7 mL
1 T	olive oil or mayonnaise	15 mL
2 T	lemon juice, freshly squeezed	30 mL
	salt and pepper, to taste	

Drain the tuna and flake it in a bowl with a fork. Add the rest of the ingredients and gently toss, blending well. *Yield: 4 servings*
    Note: to make this Italian-style, use 1 T (15 mL) olive oil and ½ t (2 mL) oregano; to make it American-style, use 1 T mayonnaise (no-fat version, to cut fat and calories).

Calories per serving: 185
Total fat: 4.0 g
Saturated fat: 0.65 g

Cholesterol: 13.1 mg
Fiber: 3.43 g
Sodium: 19.1 mg

Hopping John

A traditional Southern favorite.

1 C	black-eyed peas	250 mL
1	small pork chop, trimmed of all visible fat	1
¼ t	liquid hickory smoke	1 mL
4 C	water	1 L
1 t	chili powder	5 mL
1	medium onion, chopped	1
2⅔ C	brown rice, cooked	680 mL

Wash and drain the beans. Combine in a casserole with the pork chop, smoke flavoring, and water; cook gently for 45 minutes; add a small amount of water as needed to keep the beans from sticking. Add the chili powder and onion. Continue simmering for 30 minutes, or until the beans are tender and most of the liquid is absorbed. Mix the cooked beans and rice together. Serve warm. *Yield: 4 servings*

Calories per serving: 254   Cholesterol: 15.8 mg
Total fat: 4.87 g   Fiber: 4.87 g
Saturated fat: 1.52 g   Sodium: 52.0 mg

Figs and Pork
Moist and delicious.

4	pork chops, trimmed	4
⅓ C	almonds, chopped	90 mL
2 T	olive oil	30 mL
1	medium onion, peeled, chopped	1
1	green pepper, seeds removed, chopped	1
1 C	ready-to-eat figs, halved	250 mL
1¼ C	low-salt chicken stock	310 mL
	salt and pepper, to taste (optional)	

Coat the pork chops with the almonds; press them well. Heat the olive oil in a frying pan and fry the pork chops for about 5 minutes on each side, or until brown. Transfer them to an ovenproof casserole dish. Add the onion and pepper to the frying pan, stirring occasionally until soft, then add the figs and chicken stock. Bring to a boil. Season to taste and pour over the chops. Cover. Cook in a 350°F (175°C) oven for 1¼ hours.

Strain the cooking liquid into a pan and boil it rapidly until it is reduced by one third. Pour back over the ingredients in the dish. Serve hot with freshly boiled brown rice. *Yield: 4 servings*

Calories per serving: 594   Cholesterol: 64.6 mg
Total fat: 29.2 g   Fiber: 11.87 g
Saturated fat: 7.21 g   Sodium: 258.2 mg

Pork Chops with Prunes

Prunes and pork roasts are a traditional combination. This recipe substitutes the quicker-cooking pork chop and increases the amount of prunes.

12	pitted prunes	12
¾ C	orange juice	190 mL
2 T	red wine vinegar	30 mL
4	pork chops, center cut, lean (about 4–5 oz, or 120–140 g, each)	4
2 T	flour	30 mL
1 T	olive oil	15 mL
1	small onion, chopped	1
½ C	low-salt chicken broth	125 mL
	salt and pepper, to taste	

Put the prunes in a saucepan, add the orange juice and vinegar, and bring to boil. Lower heat and cook, uncovered, for 15 minutes. Remove from the heat. Coat the chops with flour. Heat the olive oil in a large skillet, add the chops, and cook over medium-high heat for 4 to 5 minutes on each side, or until golden brown. Remove the chops from the pan and pour off any remaining fat from the skillet. Over medium heat, sauté the onion until softened. Add the chicken stock and heat. Scrape the pan as the liquid is heated. Add the prunes and cook until the sauce has been thickened. Return the chops to skillet, stir them around the sauce just to heat, season to taste. *Yield: 4 servings*

Calories per serving: 345
Total fat: 18.4 g
Saturated fat: 5.82 g

Cholesterol: 63.6 mg
Fiber: 2.80 g
Sodium: 126.9 mg

Strawberry Muffins
Elegant enough for afternoon tea; easy enough to make for everyday breakfast.

2¼ C	oat bran cereal	560 mL
1 T	baking soda	15 mL
¼ C	dark corn syrup	60 mL
¼ C	skim milk	60 mL
¾ C	strawberry daiquiri margarita mix (non-alcoholic)	190 mL
¾ C	strawberries, fresh or frozen	190 mL
1	egg or equivalent egg substitute	1
2 T	olive oil	30 mL

Mix the dry ingredients in a large bowl. Mix the corn syrup, milk, strawberry daiquiri mix, strawberries, egg, and oil in a bowl or blender, reserving 12 strawberries for the top of the muffins. Combine with the dry ingredients and mix. Let stand 15–20 minutes. Line muffin tins with paper baking cups and fill with batter. Place a piece of strawberry on top of each and bake in a 425°F (220°C) oven for 17 minutes. Serve with strawberry preserves. *Yield: 12 servings*

Calories: 155
Total fat: 3.4 g
Saturated fat: 0.31 g

Cholesterol: 0.1 mg
Fiber: 0.20 g
Sodium: 302.0 mg

Fruity Bran Muffins

Dried fruit adds a delightful taste to these bran muffins.

⅔ C	flour	180 mL
2½ t	baking powder	12 mL
	salt, to taste	
2	egg whites, beaten	2
1 T	corn syrup	15 mL
½ C	skim milk	125 mL
2 T	olive oil	30 mL
1½ C	bran flakes	375 mL
½ C	raisins or chopped dried apricots	125 mL

Mix the flour, baking powder, and salt. In a separate bowl, combine the egg whites, corn syrup, olive oil, and milk. Add the flour mixture and mix only enough to dampen flour; the mixture will be lumpy. Fold in the cereal and raisins. Fill the muffin tins coated with non-stick cooking spray two-thirds full. Bake at 425°F (220°C) for 15–20 minutes. Delicious served with jelly. *Yield: 8 servings*

Calories per muffin: 139
Total fat: 3.5 g
Saturated fat: 0.49 g

Cholesterol: 0.3 mg
Fiber: 2.33 g
Sodium: 277.2 mg

Amazing Bran Muffins

These muffins are amazing because the batter will keep for up to six weeks in the refrigerator.

1 box (16 oz)	bran flakes	1 box (450 g)
5 C	flour	1.25 L
	salt, to taste	
5 t	baking soda	25 mL
2 C	corn syrup	500 mL
4	eggs or equivalent egg substitute, beaten	4
¾ C	olive oil	190 mL
1 qt	buttermilk	1 L

In a large bowl combine the flour, salt, and baking soda. Mix well. Stir in the bran flakes. In another bowl mix the wet ingredients. Pour the wet ingredients into the dry ones. Fill muffin tins coated with non-stick cooking spray until they are two-thirds full. Bake at 350°F (175°C) for 20 to 25 minutes until golden brown. Remove from tins and cool. *Yield: 48 muffins*

Calories per muffin: 156	Cholesterol: 0.8 mg
Total fat: 3.7 g	Fiber: 1.94 g
Saturated fat: 0.57 g	Sodium: 277.6 mg

Applesauce Bran Muffins

Store-bought bran muffins may have fiber, but these muffins also have the laxative power of apples.

1½ C	100% bran cereal	375 mL
1 C	skim milk	250 mL
2	egg whites, slightly beaten	2
½ C	applesauce, unsweetened	125 mL
2 T	olive oil	30 mL
1 C	white flour	250 mL
2½ t	baking powder	12 mL
2 T	dark corn syrup	30 mL

Combine the bran cereal and milk in a large bowl and set aside. In a separate bowl, combine the egg whites, applesauce, and oil. Add the dry ingredients. Stir this into the cereal mixture, until just blended. Fill muffin tins coated with non-stick cooking spray two-thirds full. Bake at 400°F (200°C) for 15–20 minutes or until browned on top. This is nice served with apple butter. *Yield: 12 muffins*

Calories per muffin: 106	Cholesterol: 0.3 mg
Total fat: 2.8 g	Fiber: 3.69 g
Saturated fat: 0.37 g	Sodium: 223.6 mg

ins

bran for its cholesterol-lowering potential. These of natural laxatives too.

1 C	... r	250 mL
1 C	oat bran	250 mL
2 t	baking powder	10 mL
2 t	cinnamon	10 mL
½ C	brown sugar	125 mL
½ C	carrots, shredded finely	125 mL
2	large tart apples (Granny Smith's are a good choice), peeled, cored and shredded finely	2
½ C	raisins	125 mL
1 C	chopped nuts (pecans are a good choice)	250 mL
3 T	olive oil	45 mL
½ C	nonfat milk	125 mL
2	eggs or equivalent egg substitute	2
2 t	vanilla extract	10 mL

Combine the flour, oat bran, baking powder, cinnamon, and brown sugar in a large bowl. In another bowl, combine all the other ingredients. Stir until well mixed. Pour the wet ingredients over the dry ones and stir until well blended, but do not overmix. Spoon the batter into muffin tins coated with non-stick cooking spray until they are two-thirds full. Bake in 375°F (190°C) oven for 15–18 minutes until lightly browned. *Yield: 16 servings*

Calories per muffin: 178
Total fat: 7.7 g
Saturated fat: 0.74 g

Cholesterol: 0.1 mg
Fiber: 1.63 g
Sodium: 73.2 mg

Ginger Muffins

These muffins don't rise as high as the ones that are nothing but
flour and air, but they are delicious and great laxatives.

¾ C	dried apricots, chopped	190 mL
¼ C	sweet sherry	60 mL
½ C	wheat bran	125 mL
½ C	white flour	125 mL
¾ C	whole wheat flour	190 mL
1 t	baking soda	5 mL
3 T	sugar	45 mL
2½ t	baking powder	12 mL
½ t	ginger, ground	2 mL
2	egg whites	2
⅓ C	margarine or butter, melted	90 mL
¾ C	nonfat milk	190 mL
1½ t	grated lemon rind	7 mL
	salt, to taste	

Soak the apricots in the sherry for 30 minutes, then drain, and
discard the liquid. Combine the dry ingredients in one bowl. In
a separate bowl, beat the egg whites until foamy. Add the margarine (or butter), milk, apricots, and lemon rind. Pour this wet
mixture over the dry mixture and moisten. Do not overmix. Fill
muffin tins coated with non-stick cooking spray two-thirds full.
Bake for 20–25 minutes, or until lightly brown, in 400°F (200°C)
oven. Remove from tins to wire racks, and serve while hot. *Yield:*
12 servings

Calories: 141
Total fat: 5.2 g
Saturated fat: 0.93 g

Cholesterol: 0.3 mg
Fiber: 2.34 g
Sodium: 196.4 mg

Peach Muffins

Don't let the long list of ingredients discourage you. These muffins are well worth the effort.

1 C	pinto beans, cooked, mashed	250 mL
2 T	olive oil	30 mL
2 T	molasses	30 mL
2	egg whites	2
1 t	vanilla extract	5 mL
2 T	nonfat yogurt	30 mL
½ C	whole wheat flour	125 mL
2 T	wheat germ	30 mL
1 t	baking powder	5 mL
1 t	baking soda	5 mL
½ t	cinnamon	2 mL
¼ t	nutmeg	1 mL
¼ t	ground cloves	1 mL
1 C	peaches, diced	250 mL
½ C	prunes, diced	125 mL
¼ C	nuts, chopped	60 mL

Put the beans in a food processor with the oil, molasses, egg whites, and vanilla, and process until the beans are mashed. In a bowl, combine the flour, wheat germ, baking powder, baking soda, and spices. Stir in the fruit and nuts. Spoon the mixture into muffin tins lined with paper or foil cups (for ease of cleaning) and bake in a 375°F (190°C) oven for 25 minutes or until toothpick inserted comes out clean. *Yield: 12 muffins*

Calories: 110
Total fat: 4.1 g
Saturated fat: 0.47 g

Cholesterol: 0 mg
Fiber: 3.28 g
Sodium: 139.5 mg

Pumpkin Muffins
Everybody loves these!

2¼ C	oat-bran cereal	560 mL
1 T	baking powder	15 mL
½ t	nutmeg	2 mL
½ t	cinnamon	2 mL
½ C	raisins	125 mL
½ C	canned pumpkin	125 mL
3 T	corn syrup	45 mL
½ C	frozen pineapple-juice concentrate	125 mL
¾ C	evaporated skim milk	190 mL
2 T	olive oil	30 mL
1	egg or equivalent egg substitute	1

Mix the oat bran, baking powder, nutmeg, and cinnamon in a large bowl. Mix all the other ingredients in a blender or food processor. Combine with the dry ingredients and stir just to blend. Do not overmix. Line muffin tins with paper baking cups. Fill the cups with batter and bake in a 425°F (220°C) oven for 17 minutes, or until a toothpick comes out dry. *Yield: 12 muffins*

Calories per muffin: 160
Total fat: 3.5 g
Saturated fat: 0.34 g

Cholesterol: 0 mg
Fiber: 0.91 g
Sodium: 114.1 mg

..n Bread

, it's practically a cake.

ℒ ℒ	boiling water	500 mL
11 oz	dates, diced	320 g
2	eggs or equivalent egg substitute	2
½ C	corn syrup	125 mL
1½ C	whole wheat flour	375 mL
2 t	baking powder	10 mL
1 t	baking soda	5 mL
2 C	white flour	500 mL
1 t	vanilla extract	5 mL
1 C	oat bran	250 mL
1 C	nuts, chopped	250 mL
	salt, to taste	

Place the dates in a bowl. Pour the boiling water over them, and let cool. In a separate bowl, beat the eggs until light and thick. Gradually beat in the corn syrup until the mixture is thick, creamy, and glossy. Sift together the whole wheat flour, baking powder, and baking soda. Fold one cup of the whole wheat flour mixture into the egg mixture. Fold half the dates into the mixture, then half the soaking water, white flour, and vanilla. Stir in the remaining flour mixture, remaining dates, and water, the bran, nuts, and salt. Turn the mixture into a 10-inch (25 cm) tube pan coated with non-stick cooking spray and floured. Bake in a 350°F (175°C) oven for 50 minutes, or until done. Cool in the pan for 20 minutes before turning out. *Yield: 16 slices*

Calories per slice: 250
Total fat: 5.3 g
Saturated fat: 0.37 g

Cholesterol: 0 mg
Fiber: 4.01 g
Sodium: 211.8 mg

Banana Nut Bread

Toast slices of banana nut bread for breakfast. If it lasts long enough, make a few slices into French toast; it's fabulous.

2 C	flour (sift before measuring)	500 mL
3 T	baking powder	45 mL
1	egg or equivalent egg substitute	1
3 T	olive oil	45 mL
2 T	corn syrup	30 mL
1 C	mashed banana	250 mL
¼ C	skim milk	60 mL
¼ C	water	60 mL
1 t	vanilla extract	5 mL
¾ C	walnuts, chopped	190 mL

Mix the flour and baking powder in a bowl. Set aside. In another bowl, beat the egg or substitute. Mix in the olive oil, corn syrup, banana, milk, water, and vanilla. Pour this wet mixture over the dry ingredients. Add the nuts and stir gently, just enough to moisten. Spoon the batter into a bread pan coated with non-stick cooking spray. Bake in a 350°F (175°C) oven for 50 to 60 minutes. Slice when cool. *Yield: 14 servings*

Calories per slice: 159
Total fat: 6.9 g
Saturated fat: 0.67 g

Cholesterol: 0.1 mg
Fiber: 1.05 g
Sodium: 14.5 mg

Cranberry Nut Bread
Served in baskets at New England restaurants.

2 C	white flour	500 mL
¾ C	sugar	190 mL
1½ t	baking powder	7 mL
½ t	baking soda	2 mL
¼ C	olive oil	60 mL
¾ C	apple cider	190 mL
1	egg or equivalent egg substitute, well beaten	1
2 C	cranberries, fresh, cut in half	500 mL
½ C	pecans, chopped	125 mL

Sift together the flour, sugar, baking powder, and baking soda. Mix in the olive oil until it resembles coarse meal. In a small bowl, combine the apple cider and egg; stir into the dry ingredients, just enough to moisten. Fold in the cranberries and nuts.

Turn the mixture into a 9 × 5 × 3 inch (23 × 13 × 7.5 cm) pan coated with non-stick cooking spray. Bake in a 350°F (175°C) oven on middle rack for 1 hour, or until a toothpick inserted in the center comes out clean. Cool in the pan for 5 minutes, then turn out onto a wire rack and continue to cool. *Yield: 1 large loaf*

Calories per slice: 205	Cholesterol: 0 mg
Total fat: 7.8 g	Fiber: 1.45 g
Saturated fat: 0.86 g	Sodium: 108.0 mg

Carrot Cornbread
Much moister than the traditional corn recipe.

1 C	flour	250 mL
1 C	cornmeal	250 mL
3 t	baking powder	15 mL
⅓ C	corn syrup	90 mL
¼ C	olive oil	60 mL
1	egg or equivalent egg substitute	1
1 C	nonfat yogurt	250 mL
2 (1½ C)	medium carrots, shredded	2 (375 mL)

Combine the dry ingredients in a large bowl. In a separate bowl, mix the corn syrup and olive oil together. Pour over the dry in- gredients and mix with a pastry blender until crumbly. Beat the egg until frothy and add to the wet mixture along with the yogurt and carrots. Pour into dry ingredients and stir just until blended. Pour into a 9-inch (23 cm) square pan coated with non-stick cooking spray. Bake for 20 minutes. Cool before serving. *Yield: 12 servings*

Calories per slice: 189　　　　Cholesterol: 0 mg
Total fat: 4.8 g　　　　　　　　Fiber: 0.95 g
Saturated fat: 0.64 g　　　　　Sodium: 138.0 mg

Squash Bread
Watch this disappear!

1½ C	white flour	375 mL
3¾ t	baking powder	18 mL
⅛ t	ground cloves	.5 mL
1 t	cinnamon	5 mL
½ t	nutmeg	2 mL
⅔ C	light corn syrup	180 mL
2 T	lemon juice	30 mL
1 T	dry sherry	15 mL
2	egg whites, beaten	2
½ lb	butternut squash, cooked, drained (⅔ C, or 180 mL, when mashed)	240 g
¼ C	olive oil	60 mL

Mix all the dry ingredients in a large bowl. In a second bowl, beat the corn syrup, lemon juice, sherry, egg whites, squash, and oil with a whisk or fork. Stir into the flour mixture until well blended. Pour the batter into a 5 × 9 (13 × 23 cm) loaf pan coated with non-stick cooking spray. Bake 1 hour, or until toothpick inserted in center comes out clean, in a 350°F (175°C) oven. *Yield: 18 servings*

Calories per slice: 110　　　　Cholesterol: 0 mg
Total fat: 3.2 g　　　　　　　　Fiber: 0.52 g
Saturated fat: 0.43 g　　　　　Sodium: 105.3 mg

Carrot Raisin Bread

Both carrots and raisins are natural laxatives. Most carrot raisin bread recipes are high in calories. We cut down on the calories and lifted the flavor.

2½ C	whole wheat flour	625 mL
3 T	baking powder	45 mL
1½ t	cinnamon	7 mL
¼ t	nutmeg	1 mL
4	eggs or equivalent egg substitute	4
2 t	lemon juice	10 mL
½ t	vanilla extract	2 mL
1 C	dark corn syrup	250 mL
¾ C	olive oil	190 mL
6	carrots, peeled, grated	6
¾ C	raisins	190 mL

Using a fork, mix the flour, baking powder, cinnamon, and nutmeg in a medium bowl. In a large bowl, beat the eggs, lemon juice, vanilla, and corn syrup with a whisk until frothy. Alternately add the flour mixture and the oil to the egg mixture. Stir in the carrots, then the raisins. Pour the batter into two 5 × 9 inch (13 × 23 cm) loaf pans coated with non-stick cooking spray. Bake for 50 minutes, or until a toothpick inserted in the center comes out clean. Allow to cool before turning out of the pans. *Yield: 36 servings*

Calories: 117
Total fat: 4.7 g
Saturated fat: 0.62 g

Cholesterol: 0 mg
Fiber: 1.70 g
Sodium: 124.0 mg

Chapter 8: Desserts

Fresh Fruit Mélange

Make this ahead of time. It's the perfect ending to a summer evening.

1	banana, peeled, cut into 1-inch (2.5 cm) rounds	1
2	apples, peeled, cored, and sliced	2
1	pear	1
3	peaches, unpeeled, pitted, and quartered	3
2	oranges, peeled and sectioned	2
1	grapefruit, peeled and sectioned	1
1 C	seedless grapes	250 mL
½ C	fruit juice (orange or pear are good choices)	125 mL
¼ C	molasses	60 mL
¼ C	lime juice	60 mL
4	cloves	4
½ t	allspice	2 mL

In a large bowl, combine the fruit. In a saucepan combine remaining ingredients. Cook over low heat 5 minutes, stirring constantly. Strain to remove the cloves. Pour the mixture over fruit. Stir to blend thoroughly. Cover and refrigerate for 4 hours. *Yield: 12 servings*

Calories per serving: 88
Total fat: 0.4 g
Saturated fat: 0.06 g

Cholesterol: 0 mg
Fiber: 2.44 g
Sodium: 3.9 mg

Elegant Almonds and Fruit

Whip this up in the morning; you'll love having it ready for dinner.

20 oz	pineapple chunks, packed in juice	600 g
16 oz	sliced peaches, fresh or canned	480 g
2 T	canola oil	30 mL
4 T	slivered almonds (unsalted)	60 mL
1 T	lemon juice	15 mL
5 T	unsweetened pineapple juice from the can of pineapple chunks	75 mL

Drain the canned fruit and save the juices. Drop the fruit into a serving bowl and refrigerate. Heat the oil in a small frying pan, then add the almonds; cook gently, stirring, until the almonds are lightly browned; remove from the heat and cool. Add the lemon juice and pineapple juice to the almonds and stir; toss over fruit. Refrigerate until serving time. This is best served chilled. *Yield: 6 servings*

Calories per serving: 156	Cholesterol: 0 mg
Total fat: 7.8 g	Fiber: 1.93 g
Saturated fat: .63 g	Sodium: 6.4 mg

Bananas Foster

Ignite this at the table the way they do in expensive restaurants.

4	ripe bananas, peeled and cut lengthwise	4
2 t	lemon juice	10 mL
¼ C	margarine or butter	60 mL
2 T	brown sugar	30 mL
dash	cinnamon	dash
1 T	white sugar	15 mL
¼ C	light rum	60 mL

Sprinkle the bananas with lemon juice. In a chafing dish melt the margarine (or butter) over low heat. Stir in the brown sugar and cinnamon. Add the bananas and cook for approximately 2 minutes, stirring without crushing the bananas. Sprinkle with sugar and add the rum. Use a long wooden match to ignite the rum. Serve as soon as the flame burns itself out. Serve with frozen yogurt or vanilla ice cream. *Yield: 4 servings*

Calories: 305	Cholesterol: 0 mg
Total fat: 11.6 g	Fiber: 2.32 g
Saturated fat: 2.39 g	Sodium: 133.2 mg

Fruit in Wine

Instead of peaches and blueberries, try strawberries with melon, pears with blueberries, cantaloupe with raspberries, or nectarines with strawberries or raspberries.

2 T	sugar	30 mL
2 T	sweet wine	30 mL
4	fresh peaches, peeled* and sliced	4
1 C	fresh or frozen blueberries	250 mL

Heat the sugar and wine in a saucepan over low heat until the sugar dissolves. Add the peaches, cover the saucepan, and simmer for approximately 5 minutes over very low heat. Stir in the blueberries. Serve hot or chilled. *Yield: 4 servings*

Calories per serving: 103	Cholesterol: 0 mg
Total fat: 0.3 g	Fiber: 2.13 g
Saturated fat: 0.01 g	Sodium: 3.8 mg

*To peel ripe fresh peaches more easily, drop them in boiling water for a minute or so to loosen the skins. If fresh peaches are out of season, substitute canned peaches and omit the cooking step.

Dessert Fruit Compote
Make this when summer fruits are at their best.

3	pears, cored and sliced	3
6	peaches, peeled, pitted, and sliced	6
1 C	peach or pear nectar	250 mL
1 pt	strawberries, hulled	500 mL
½ C	pineapple juice	125 mL
2 t	lemon juice	10 mL
1 t	cinnamon	5 mL
1	lime, cut into wedges	1

Combine all the ingredients in a saucepan. Cook over low heat for 5 minutes, stirring occasionally. Cover and chill for 2 hours. *Yield: 12 servings*

Calories per serving: 70
Total fat: 0.3 g
Saturated fat: 0.02 g

Cholesterol: 0 mg
Fiber: 2.67 g
Sodium: 2.0 mg

Mock Champagne and Fresh Fruit
Champagne can also be used in place of diet soda.

8 oz	diet soda such as strawberry or lemon-lime	250 g
4 C	fresh fruit, such as strawberries, blueberries, or diced peaches	1 L
2 t	lemon juice	10 mL
1 T	sugar	15 mL

Chill the champagne or soda. Meanwhile, combine the pieces of fruit in a bowl and sprinkle them with lemon juice to prevent their darkening. Sprinkle sugar over the fruit and stir; chill. To serve, place one quarter of the fruit in each of four pretty glass dishes. Pour the champagne or diet soda over the fruit. *Yield: 4 servings*

Calories per serving: 57
Total fat: 0.6 g
Saturated fat: 0.03 g

Cholesterol: 0 mg
Fiber: 3.14 g
Sodium: 5.5 mg

Baked Apples

4	apples	4
4 t	margarine or butter	20 mL
8 t	sugar	40 mL
4 dashes	cinnamon	4 dashes
4 dashes	nutmeg	4 dashes

Use a small paring knife to core the apples. Discard the core, seeds, and top of the peel. Set the apples in a baking pan lined with aluminum foil, to make the cleanup easier. Drop 1 teaspoon (5 mL) margarine (or butter), 2 teaspoons (10 mL) sugar, and dash of cinnamon and nutmeg in the center of each apple. Bake in a 350°F (175°C) oven for approximately 40 minutes. *Yield: 4 servings*

Calories per serving: 376
Total fat: 22.9 g
Saturated fat: 4.60 g

Cholesterol: 0 mg
Fiber: 3.75 g
Sodium: 260.9 mg

Yummy Fried Apples
The name says it all.

2 T	margarine or butter	30 mL
2 T	brown sugar	30 mL
¼ t	cinnamon	1 mL
dash	nutmeg	dash
4	medium apples, unpeeled and cored, thinly sliced	4

Melt the margarine (or butter) in a large skillet over low heat. Stir in the brown sugar, cinnamon, and nutmeg. Add the apple slices. Cook gently for 5 minutes. Stir occasionally. *Yield: 4 servings*

Calories per serving: 156
Total fat: 6.1 g
Saturated fat: 1.18 g

Cholesterol: 0 mg
Fiber: 3.65 g
Sodium: 66.1 mg

Bananas in Rum Sauce

The orange adds a bright flavor to this version.

2 T	olive oil	30 mL
6	bananas, peeled and split lengthwise	6
1	orange, peeled and sectioned	1
¼ C	rum	60 mL
2 t	brown sugar	10 mL

Heat the olive oil in a large skillet. Place the bananas cut-side down and cook over a low heat for 1 minute. Add the orange sections. Cook for 3 minutes more, turning the oranges occasionally. Pour in the rum and ignite. After the flame is extinguished, sprinkle the brown sugar over the fruit, stirring gently to combine.
Yield: 12 servings

Calories per serving: 102	Cholesterol: 0 mg
Total fat: 2.5 g	Fiber: 1.46 g
Saturated fat: 0.41 g	Sodium: 0.7 mg

Apple-Cranberry Crunch

A family favorite. Make it on a fall Sunday afternoon while soup is simmering on the stove.

Filling

3 C	Macintosh apples, coarsely chopped, unpeeled	750 mg
2 C	cranberries, fresh or frozen	500 mL
¾ C	sugar	190 mL

Topping

1½ C	old-fashioned oats	375 mL
¾ C	pecans, chopped	190 mL
½ C	light brown sugar	125 mL
⅓ C	all-purpose flour	90 mL
¼ C	margarine or butter, melted	60 mL
¼ C	olive oil	60 mL

To make the filling: Mix all the filling ingredients in a medium bowl. Turn into ungreased 2½ quart (2.5 L) round baking dish or 9-inch (23 cm) deep dish pie plate.

To make the topping: Mix the oats, pecans, brown sugar, and flour. Stir in the margarine (or butter) and olive oil until blended. Crumble over the filling; press down lightly. Bake in a 350°F (175°C) oven for 45 minutes, or until the topping is browned and the filling is bubbling. *Yield: 9 servings*

Calories: 387
Total fat: 18.3 g
Saturated fat: 18.3 g

Cholesterol: 0 mg
Fiber: 4.44 g
Sodium: 4.7 mg

Apple Crisp
Our children's favorite!

4 C	apples, sliced	1 L
¼ C	water	60 mL
1 T	molasses	15 mL
2 t	brown sugar	10 mL
1 T	lemon juice	15 mL
1 t	cinnamon	5 mL
¼ t	cloves	1 mL
¾ C	rolled oats	190 mL

Combine the apples, water, molasses, brown sugar, lemon juice, cinnamon, and cloves. Mix well. Arrange the apple mixture in an 8-inch (20 cm) square baking dish coated with non-stick cooking spray. Combine the remaining ingredients and sprinkle them over the apples. Bake for 30 minutes, or until the apples are tender and the topping is lightly browned. *Yield: 8 servings*

Calories per serving: 121
Total fat: 1.0 g
Saturated fat: 0.20 g

Cholesterol: 0 mg
Fiber: 4.09 g
Sodium: 2.0 mg

rumble

... easy to make as a non-laxative box cake.

⅓ C	white flour	90 mL
⅓ C	whole wheat flour	90 mL
⅓ C	bran	90 mL
½ C	almonds, ground	125 mL
⅓ C	margarine or butter, diced	90 mL
¼ C	brown sugar	60 mL
¾ lb	cooking apples, unpeeled, cored, and sliced	350 g
¾ lb	raspberries	350 g
½ C	brown sugar	125 mL
3 T	water	45 mL
¼ C	slivered almonds	60 mL

Pour flours, bran, and almonds into a bowl. Cut in the margarine (or butter) until the mixture resembles bread crumbs. Stir in the sugar. Put the apple slices in a baking dish coated with non-stick cooking spray. Top with the raspberries, sugar, and water. Add the flour mixture over the fruit and sprinkle with slivered almonds. Bake in a 400°F (200°C) oven for 40 minutes, or until golden brown. Serve hot. _Yield: 6 servings_

Calories per serving: 417
Total fat: 19.1 g
Saturated fat: 2.79 g

Cholesterol: 0 mg
Fiber: 7.61 g
Sodium: 125.0 mg

Triple Pear Crisp

Dried pears, pear juice, and fresh pears make the triple.
Unbelievably laxative, easy to make, and delicious make a triple,
too!

6 oz	dried pears, cored, and chopped, stems discarded	180 g
1 C	pear juice, bottled	250 mL
4 C	pears, fresh, chopped into bite-sized pieces, cored (4 or 5 medium pears)	1 L
½ C	olive oil	125 mL
⅓ C	molasses	90 mL
2 C	rolled oats	500 mL
1 t	cinnamon	5 mL
½ t	nutmeg	2 mL

Bring the dried pears and pear juice to a boil in a small saucepan. Reduce the heat and simmer until the pears are tender, about 10 minutes. Put the pears in an 8-inch (20 cm) square baking dish. In a separate bowl, mix the fresh pears, olive oil, molasses, oats, cinnamon, and nutmeg, evenly coating the oats. Pour the tender pears and cooking liquid over the fresh pears. Spread the oat mixture on top.

Bake in a 375°F (190°C) oven for 35 minutes, or until the topping is brown and crisp. *Yield: 6 servings*

Calories per serving: 467
Total fat: 20.3 g
Saturated fat: 2.91 g

Cholesterol: 0 mg
Fiber: 7.30 g
Sodium: 24.4 mg

Poached Pears in Raspberry Sauce

Easy—but fancy enough to rival desserts served in gourmet restaurants.

2 C	wine (sweet is best)	500 mL
3 C	water	750 mL
1½ C	frozen apple juice concentrate	375 mL
2 sticks	cinnamon	2 sticks
½ t	ginger	2 mL
¼ t	nutmeg, ground	1 mL
6	pears, firm, cored from the bottom, stem intact	6
1½ C	fresh raspberries, or frozen, without sugar syrup	375 mL
¼ C	water	60 mL
2 T	cornstarch	30 mL
	fresh mint for garnish (optional)	

In a saucepan, bring the wine, 3 cups (750 mL) water, and 1 cup (250 mL) apple juice concentrate to a boil. Add the cinnamon, ginger, and nutmeg. Reduce the heat to a simmer and drop in the pears. Cook until tender, about 20–35 minutes. The pears are done when a knife can easily be inserted into them; but do not overcook.

Remove the pears and put them into individual dishes. Discard the cinnamon sticks, measure out 3 cups of cooking liquid. Add the remaining ½ cup (125 mL) apple juice concentrate to the cooking liquid, return the mixture to the pan, and boil about 15 minutes, until it is reduced to half its original volume (to just under 2 cups).

Reduce the heat to a simmer and add the raspberries, reserving a few for garnish. In a small bowl, stir together ¼ cup water and the cornstarch. Remove the cooking liquid from the heat and slowly add the cornstarch, stirring constantly. Over low heat, stir until the sauce thickens. Strain if you want to remove the raspberry seeds. Pour the sauce over the pears. Serve warm or chilled. *Yield: 6 servings*

Calories per serving: 302	Cholesterol: 0 mg
Total fat: 1.0 g	Fiber: 6.52 g
Saturated fat: 0.08 g	Sodium: 5.8 mg

Pears Baked with Figs
Very high in natural laxative power. Delicious too.

2 (1 lb)	ripe Anjou pears	2 (500 g)
16 (8 oz)	figs or figlets, dried	16 (250 g)
1 T	orange juice	15 mL
1 T	lemon juice	15 mL
¾ C	water	190 mL
1 T	apricot preserves	15 mL
½ C	vanilla nonfat yogurt (optional)	125 mL

Halve and core the pears. Cut the figs crosswise into slices and arrange them in a shallow ovenproof dish. Place the pears, flat-side down, on top of the figs. In a small bowl, mix together the water, lemon juice, orange juice, and preserves. Pour over the pears. Cover with foil. Bake the pears in a 350°F (175°C) oven for 45 minutes. Check during baking and add up to ½ cup (125 mL) extra water, if necessary, to keep the pears moist. Cool and serve at room temperature. Serve with yogurt, if desired. *Yield: 4 servings*

Calories per serving: 318
Total fat: 1.4 g
Saturated fat: 0.22 g

Cholesterol: 0 mg
Fiber: 12.99 g
Sodium: 29.7 mg

New Hampshire Yogurt Treat
Nothing could be easier!

½ C	walnuts, chopped	125 mL
5 T	maple syrup, chilled	75 mL
2 C	nonfat yogurt, chilled	500 mL

Stir the walnuts into the syrup in a small bowl. Place the yogurt in a separate bowl. Pour the syrup-nut mixture over the yogurt. With a spoon, swirl the mixture in but do not mix. *Yield: 6 servings*

Calories per serving: 147
Total fat: 5.2 g
Saturated fat: 0.47 g

Cholesterol: 0 mg
Fiber: 0.43 g
Sodium: 51.1 mg

Prune Pudding

Prune pudding is a fondly remembered favorite in many households.

1 C	pitted prunes	250 mL
1¼ C	water	300 mL
½ C	nonfat cottage cheese	125 mL
⅔ C	nonfat yogurt	180 mL
3 T	orange juice	45 mL
½ t	lemon extract	2 mL
2 T	brown sugar	30 mL
2	egg whites	2
3 T	almonds, slivered, lightly toasted	45 mL

Simmer the prunes in a pan with water to cover over until the fruit is tender, about 15 minutes. Puree the prunes with any remaining liquid in the pan. Set aside. Combine the cottage cheese, yogurt, orange juice, and lemon extract in a blender. Add the brown sugar and prune puree, and blend. With an electric mixer, beat the egg whites until stiff. Fold the beaten egg whites into the blended ingredients. Put one quarter of the mixture in each of four glass serving dishes and chill. Sprinkle with slivered almonds. *Yield: 4 servings*

Calories per serving: 217
Total fat: 3.4 g
Saturated fat: 0.32 g

Cholesterol: 2.5 mg
Fiber: 4.38 g
Sodium: 51.2 mg

Cranberry and Prune Whip

Make this while dinner's cooking. Your family will love it. (No one will suspect it's a natural laxative.)

1 C	pitted prunes	250 mL
2 C	apple juice	500 mL
1 C	whole berry cranberry sauce	250 mL
2	egg whites	2
	salt, to taste (optional)	
¼ C	chopped nuts (optional)	60 mL

Cook the prunes in apple juice until plump and very soft. Drain. Using a food processor with a knife blade or a blender, chop the prunes. Then mix in the cranberries and blend until smooth. In an electric mixer, beat the egg whites and salt until the whites are stiff. Add the fruit mixture, a small portion at a time (beating will increase the volume of the mixture). Fold in the nuts (optional) and chill. *Yield: 7 servings*

Calories per serving: 143   Cholesterol: 0 mg
Total fat: 0.1 g   Fiber: 2.21 g
Saturated fat: 0.02 g   Sodium: 27.7 mg

Prune and Apricot Frozen Dessert

Packed with natural laxative power, this dessert is a low-calorie substitute for ice cream.

2 C	grape juice	500 mL
½ C	dried pitted prunes, freshly cooked	125 mL
½ C	dried apricots, freshly cooked	125 mL
1 T	lemon juice	15 mL
2 C	vanilla nonfat yogurt	500 mL

Cook the prunes and apricots in the grape juice until plump, about 20 minutes. Drain. Add the lemon juice. Puree in a blender or food processor. Fold in the yogurt. Pour into an ice cube tray and freeze to mush. Remove, beat well, and return the mixture to the freezer compartment until ready to serve. This is best if made about 2 hours before serving. *Yield: 8 servings*

Calories per serving: 65   Cholesterol: 0 mg
Total fat: 0 g   Fiber: 1.53 g
Saturated fat: 0 g   Sodium: 36.6 mg

Prune Yogurt

Cooking the prunes in apple juice makes them moist and flavorful.

1 C	dried prunes	250 mL
1 C	apple juice	250 mL
1 C	nonfat yogurt	250 mL

Place prunes in a small heavy-bottomed saucepan. Add the apple juice. Bring the mixture to a boil. Reduce heat, cover, and simmer for 15 minutes. Drain the prunes, saving the liquid. Put the prunes and ¼-cup (60 mL) cooking liquid into blender or food processor. Blend at high speed for 30 seconds. Cool. Fold into yogurt. *Yield: 2 servings*

Calories per serving: 311
Total fat: 0.2 g
Saturated fat: 0.03 g

Cholesterol: 0 mg
Fiber: 7.93 g
Sodium: 76.0 mg

Mock Plum Pudding

This takes only a few minutes to make, but it tastes like the all-day version my grandmother used to make.

1 pkg. (3 oz)	sugar-free raspberry gelatin	1 pkg. (90 g)
½ C	raisins	125 mL
1 box (8 oz)	dates	1 box (225 g)
¼ C	walnuts, chopped	60 mL
1 C	Grape-Nuts cereal	250 mL
¾ C	rhubarb pieces, cooked in water for 5 minutes	190 mL
½ t	cinnamon	2 mL
½ t	nutmeg	2 mL

Mix the gelatin as directed on the package. Stir in the remaining ingredients and chill until firm, 2 to 3 hours. *Yield: 9 servings*

Calories per serving: 186
Total fat: 1.8 g
Saturated fat: 0.20 g

Cholesterol: 0 mg
Fiber: 3.91 g
Sodium: 88.7 mg

Creamy Bread Pudding with Pumpkin

Have you noticed bread pudding reappearing on restaurant menus? This is a fabulous and highly laxative version.

8 slices	whole wheat or high-fiber bread	8 slices
6	egg whites	6
1 T	olive oil	15 mL
2¼ C	skim milk	560 mL
1 can	pumpkin	1 can
(16 oz)		(450 g)
¼ C	molasses	60 mL
¾ C	sugar	190 mL
1½ t	cinnamon	7 mL
1½ t	pumpkin pie spice	7 mL
½ t	nutmeg	2 mL
1 t	vanilla	5 mL
¾ C	raisins	190 mL

Crumble the bread by hand or with a blender or food processor. Combine the egg whites, oil, milk, pumpkin, molasses, sugar, spices, and vanilla. Add raisins, then combine with the bread crumbs in a 2-quart (2 L) casserole coated with non-stick cooking spray. Set the casserole dish into a larger baking dish partially filled with hot water. Bake in a 375°F (190°C) oven for one hour, or until a knife inserted comes out clean. *Yield: 12 servings*

Calories per serving: 169
Total fat: 1.8 g
Saturated fat: 0.25 g

Cholesterol: 0.8 mg
Fiber: 3.11 g
Sodium: 54.1 mg

⌣ berry Pudding

Fresh or frozen cranberries work equally well. Everyone loves this pudding.

4 C	cranberries	1 L
1 C	sugar	250 mL
4	eggs, or equivalent egg substitute	4
2 C	corn syrup	500 mL
2 C	flour	500 mL
1 C	margarine or butter, melted	250 mL
¼ C	olive oil	60 mL

Spread the cranberries over the bottom of a 9 × 13 inch (23 × 33 cm) pan and sprinkle with the sugar. In a medium bowl, beat the eggs well. Add the corn syrup and beat until thoroughly mixed. Add the flour, melted margarine (or butter), and oil. Beat well. Pour over the top of the cranberries. Bake at 350°F (175°C) for 50 minutes. *Yield: 12 servings*

Calories: 495	Cholesterol: 0 mg
Total fat: 19.5 g	Fiber: 1.77 g
Saturated fat: 3.37 g	Sodium: 80.9 mg

Cooked Date Pudding

A real pudding cooked the old-fashioned way. One of our friends, Millard, liked this dessert the best.

½ C	molasses	125 mL
½ C	whole wheat flour	125 mL
	salt, to taste	
½ C	cold water	125 mL
2 C	boiling water	500 mL
¾ C	dates, pitted, diced	190 mL
	vanilla- or fruit-flavored nonfat yogurt	

Combine the molasses, flour, and salt in the top of a double boiler and mix well. Stir in the cold water. Stir in the boiling water gradually and cook over direct heat until the mixture thickens, stirring constantly. Add the dates. Place over simmering water, cover, and cook about one and one-quarter hours, stirring occasionally. Cool and chill. Serve with yogurt or cardamom cream, which is made by mixing powdered cardamom and heavy cream. *Yield: 4 servings*

Calories per serving: 228   Cholesterol: 0 mg
Total fat: 0.3 g   Fiber: 4.55 g
Saturated fat: 0 g   Sodium: 426.3 mg

Apricot-Pear Topping
Serve with corncakes, stirred into vanilla yogurt, or as a dessert sauce.

2 C	water	500 mL
1 C	corn syrup	250 mL
2 t	lemon juice	10 mL
1 t	vanilla extract	5 mL
3	pears, diced	3
1 can	apricot halves, including	1 can
(16 oz)	liquid	(450 g)
¼ C	pear or apricot juice	60 mL
⅛ t	nutmeg	.5 mL
2 t	cornstarch	10 mL
	vanilla nonfat yogurt (optional)	

Combine the water, corn syrup, lemon juice, and vanilla in a medium saucepan. Cook over medium heat, stirring until mixed. Add the pears. Bring to a boil, reduce heat, cover, and simmer for 30 minutes. Set aside. Place the apricots and the remaining ingredients in a blender or food processor. Puree until smooth. In a second saucepan, pour the apricot mixture. Cook over medium heat, stirring constantly until thickened. Add the pear mixture. Cook 5 minutes over medium heat, stirring constantly. *Yield: 8 servings*

Calories per serving: 222 g   Cholesterol: 0 mg
Total fat: 0.35 g   Fiber: 5.48 g
Saturated fat: 0.02 g   Sodium: 60.6 mg

Apricot Mould

Can't be beat for a cool summer dessert.

1 can (10 oz)	crushed pineapple	1 can (280 g)
1 can (15 oz)	apricots	1 can (420 g)
1 can (5½ oz)	mandarin oranges	1 can (150 g)
2 pkg. (each 3 oz)	orange gelatin	2 pkg. (100 g each)
2 C	boiling water	500 mL
1 C	cold water	250 mL
1 C	vanilla-flavored nonfat yogurt	250 mL

Drain the fruit well. Crush the apricots and combine the fruit. Dissolve the gelatin in the hot water and add the cold water. Stir the gelatin and yogurt into the fruit. Pour into a 10-cup (2.5 L) mould and refrigerate until set. *Yield: 8 servings*

Calories per serving: 165
Total fat: 0.5 g
Saturated fat: 0.26 g

Cholesterol: 1.9 mg
Fiber: 0.88 g
Sodium: 28.8 mg

Apricot Pudding

Foolproof and elegant.

3 C	dried apricots	750 mL
1¼ C	water	310 mL
2 T	fresh orange juice	30 mL
½ C	nonfat yogurt	125 mL
3	egg whites	3
½ t	almond extract	2 mL
	sweetener, to taste	

Soak the apricots in water for a few hours, then gently cook them until tender. Blend them with fresh orange juice and yogurt until smooth. Whisk the egg whites until stiff; fold into the apricot mixture. Sweeten to taste and serve in individual dishes. *Yield: 4 servings*

Calories per serving: 186
Total fat: 0 g
Saturated fat: 0 g

Cholesterol: 0 mg
Fiber: 6.64 g
Sodium: 5.52 mg

Rhubarb Delight

Rhubarb is considered by some experts to be among the most laxative foods.

5 C	rhubarb, cut into small pieces	1.25 L
½ C	sugar	125 mL
½ C	water	125 mL
1 C	whole wheat flour	250 mL
½ C	sugar	125 mL
1 t	baking powder	5 mL
3	egg whites	3

Put the rhubarb in a large baking dish. Combine it with ½ cup (125 mL) sugar. In another small bowl, combine the flour, ½ cup (125 mL) sugar, baking powder, and egg whites. Place small spoonfuls of dough onto the rhubarb. Bake in a 350°F (175°C) oven for about 45–55 minutes. *Yield: 8 servings*

Calories per serving: 165
Total fat: 0.4 g
Saturated fat: 0.01 g

Cholesterol: 0 mg
Fiber: 3.27 g
Sodium: 71.9 mg

↑pple Spice Cake

Beans in a cake? Yes. They add wonderful moistness and lots of laxative power.

2 C	cooked or canned navy beans, drained and pureed	500 mL
1	egg or equivalent egg substitute, beaten	1
¼ C	olive oil	60 mL
1 C	all-purpose flour	250 mL
1 t	baking soda	5 mL
1 C	sugar	250 mL
1 t	cinnamon	5 mL
1 t	allspice	5 mL
½ t	ground cloves	2 mL
2 C	apples, chopped	500 mL
½ C	pecans	125 mL
1 C	raisins or currants	250 mL
2 t	vanilla extract	10 mL
	confectioners' sugar	
8	walnut halves (optional)	8

Mix the beans, egg, and olive oil in an electric mixer. In another bowl, mix the flour, sugar, baking soda, cinnamon, allspice, and ground cloves. Add this to the bean mixture and stir by hand until combined. Add the apples, chopped walnuts, raisins, and vanilla. Stir until well blended.

Pour the mixture into a tube pan and bake in the center of a 375°F (190°C) oven for 45 minutes to an hour. Turn out onto wire rack to cool. Dust with confectioners' sugar and, if desired, decorate with walnut halves. *Yield: 20 servings*

Calories per slice: 170.5	Cholesterol: 0 mg
Total fat: 5.7 g	Fiber: 2.15 g
Saturated fat: .65 g	Sodium: 85.45 mg

Ginger Cake
A delicious variation on traditional gingerbread.

1 C	molasses	250 mL
4	eggs, or equivalent egg substitute	4
¾ C	olive oil	190 mL
2 C	white kidney beans (cannellini), pureed*	500 mL
2 t	baking soda	10 mL
1 C	flour	250 mL
2 t	cinnamon	10 mL
1 t	ginger	5 mL
½ t	nutmeg	2 mL
1 C	pecans, chopped	250 mL
2 C	grated carrots (3 medium)	500 mL
½ C	raisins**	125 mL

Using an electric mixer, beat the molasses and eggs in a large bowl. Beat the oil into the egg mixture and slowly mix in the bean puree, baking soda, cinnamon, ginger, and nutmeg. With a spatula, fold in the nuts, raisins, and carrots. Pour everything into a 9 × 13 (23 × 33) (lasagna) pan coated with non-stick cooking spray. Cook in the center of a 350°F (175°C) oven for 1 hour and 55 minutes. Cool on a wire rack before cutting. *Yield: 16 servings*

Calories per slice: 292.5	Cholesterol: 0 mg
Total fat: 15.25 g	Fiber: 2.91 g
Saturated fat: 1.8 g	Sodium: 402 mg

*Start with 4 C (1 L) drained beans.
**Diced apricots can be substituted for raisins.

Prune and Raisin Pie

*Because this recipe calls for ingredients usually at hand, it's
great to put together on the spur of the moment.*

Crust

2 T	margarine or butter	30 mL
1 T	honey	15 mL
3 T	light corn syrup	45 mL
1½ C	rolled oats	375 mL
¼ C	walnuts, chopped finely	60 mL

Filling

1 C	raisins	250 mL
1 C	prunes, cut into small pieces	250 mL
1	lemon, finely grated rind and juice	1
2 T	brown sugar	30 mL
¼ t	cinnamon	1 mL
¼ t	nutmeg	1 mL
⅔ C	water	190 mL
1 T	cornstarch	15 mL
2	egg whites	2
pinch	cream of tartar	pinch
2 T	sugar	30 mL
⅓ C	slivered almonds	90 mL

To make the crust: In a large pan, melt the margarine (or butter)
with the honey and corn syrup. Remove from heat and stir in the
oats and walnuts until the mixture binds. Press into an 8-inch (20
cm) shallow cake tin to make an even shell. Chill while making
filling.

To make the filling: Put the raisins, prunes, lemon rind and juice,
sugar, spice, and water in a saucepan, bring to a boil, and simmer
for 5 minutes. Moisten the cornstarch in a little cold water, add
it to the saucepan, and bring to a boil, stirring constantly. Reduce
the heat and simmer 1 minute. Pour into cake tin. Beat the egg
whites, cream of tartar, and sugar until stiff and spread carefully
over the raisin-prune mixture. Sprinkle with almonds. Bake in a

350°F (175°C) oven for about 20 minutes, or until the top is golden. *Yield: 8 servings*

Calories per slice: 311	Cholesterol: 0 mg
Total fat: 8.6 g	Fiber: 4.95 g
Saturated fat: 1.26 g	Sodium: 54.5 mg

Basic Pie Shell

We added a little wheat bran to increase the fiber, and it increased the flavor too.

1 C	white flour	250 mL
¼ C	wheat bran	60 mL
	salt, to taste (optional)	
6 T	shortening	90 mL
3 T	cold water	45 mL

Combine the flour, bran, and salt. Cut the shortening into the flour mixture until the mixture forms crumbs. Add cold water 1 table-spoon (15 mL) at a time and form into a ball. Chill for at least 1 hour. Roll to fit 9-inch (23 cm) pie plate. To bake unfilled, prick the crust with a fork and fill with dry "baking" beans (so it will keep its shape; remove the "beans" after baking). Bake at 425°F (220°C) for 10 minutes, or until lightly browned. Double the recipe for a two-crust pie. *Yield: 8 servings*

Calories for ⅛ of one layer crust: 156	Cholesterol: 0 mg
Total fat: 9.9 g	Fiber: 1.35 g
Saturated fat: 2.95 g	Sodium: 2.9 mg

Blueberry Pie Filling

Some of the blueberries are cooked and some are left raw. That makes for the best blueberry pie you've ever tasted.

¾ C	sugar	190 mL
3 T	cornstarch	45 mL
¼ C	water	60 mL
4 C	blueberries	1 L
1 T	lemon juice	15 mL

Combine the sugar and cornstarch in a saucepan. Add the water and 2 cups (500 mL) blueberries. Over medium heat, bring the mixture to boil, stirring constantly. It will become thick and clear. Remove it from the heat and add the lemon juice. Cool. Place the remaining 2 cups (500 mL) raw blueberries into a 9-inch (23 cm) pie shell. Top with cooked mixture. Chill. *Yield: 8 servings*

Calories for ⅛ of filling
   only: 121
Total fat: 0.3 g
Saturated fat: 0.01 g

Cholesterol: 0 mg
Fiber: 1.67 g
Sodium: 5.1 mg

Apple Pie Filling

This pie filling has extra laxative boosters—almonds and whole wheat bread crumbs.

3	cooking apples, large, unpeeled, cored and chopped	3
1½ C	fresh whole wheat bread crumbs	310 mL
1 T	lemon juice	15 mL
½ C	corn syrup	125 mL
2 T	margarine or butter, melted	30 mL
½ C	almonds, chopped	125 mL

Mix together all the ingredients. Spoon into a prepared 9-inch (23 cm) pie crust. Bake in a 350°F (175°C) oven for about 50 minutes. *Yield: 8 servings*

Calories per serving: 117   Cholesterol: 0 mg
Total fat: 5.7 g   Fiber: 2.64 g
Saturated fat: 0.61 g   Sodium: 12.0 mg

Index

About the Authors

Karin Cadwell received her bachelor's and master's degrees in nursing from the University of Pennsylvania and a Ph.D. in Health Policy from The Union Institute. She also has a bachelor's degree in English from Upsala College. Currently living on Cape Cod with her husband, eight cats, and two dogs, Karin enjoys entertaining, especially when her two grown daughters, Kajsa and Anna, come home with carloads of friends. In order to accommodate the special dietary needs of friends and family, she has learned to create delicious dishes that are enjoyed by everyone, both those with and those without health concerns.

Edith White has managed to combine her two loves, cooking and teaching, in the form of cookbook writing. A professional educator with a bachelor's degree from Tufts University and a master's from the University of Illinois, she learned the basics of cooking from her mother. Since her children, Andrew, Christopher, and Amy, are now young adults and out of the house, she no longer has a regular audience for her culinary skills, but she enjoys entertaining friends as often as possible. She lives on Cape Cod near the ocean in a cottage that belonged to her grandmother.

Karin and Edith are the authors of two other books published by Sterling—*The Complete Low-Sodium/Low-Salt Cookbook* and *The Complete Low Sodium/Low Cholesterol Cookbook*, and the soon-to-be-published *Great Diabetic Desserts and Sweets*. Members of the faculty of Health Education Associates, Inc., Sandwich, Massachusetts, they both instruct nurses, nutritionists, and physicians in continuing-education courses nationwide.